# HOME OFFICE
# SOLUTIONS

*How to Set Up an Efficient Workspace Anywhere in Your House*

# HOME OFFICE SOLUTIONS

*How to Set Up an Efficient Workspace Anywhere in Your House*

CRE**A**TIVE
HOMEOWNER®

**CHRIS PETERSON**

# CRE▲TIVE
## HOMEOWNER®

**Home Office Solutions**
Editor: Colleen Dorsey
Copy Editor: Amy Deputato
Designer: Chris Morrison
Indexer: Jay Kreider

ISBN 978-1-58011-859-0

Library of Congress Control Number: 2020942772

We are always looking for talented authors. To submit an idea, please send a brief inquiry to acquisitions@foxchapelpublishing.com.

Printed in the United States of America

Current Printing (last digit)
10 9 8 7 6 5 4 3 2 1

Creative Homeowner®, *www.creativehomeowner.com*, is an imprint of New Design Originals Corporation and distributed exclusively in North America by Fox Chapel Publishing Company, Inc., 800-457-9112, 903 Square Street, Mount Joy, PA 17552, and in the United Kingdom by Grantham Book Service, Trent Road, Grantham, Lincolnshire, NG31 7XQ.

# CONTENTS

# INTRODUCTION

Setting up your home office thoughtfully and with a modicum of advance planning is the way to avoid the downsides and maximize the benefits of working from home.

Chances are you have everything you need to work from your home or apartment. The big challenge is carving out the ideal workspace. The perfect home office combines comfort and efficiency, inspires productivity, and adds to—rather than detracts from—the home environment. A great home office design achieves balance and helps the worker do the same.

Home and office, relaxation and work: these can seem like daunting and sometimes competing goals, but this book can help you achieve them. Whether you're a customer service representative who does most of your work on a computer, an editor who works mostly with physical printouts, or a lawyer who goes about the bulk of your business on the phone or by way of video, this book contains all the information you need to create a comfortable, customized workspace that fosters creativity and productivity. Use the information here to create a home office that does everything you need it to do, in exactly the ways you need to accommodate your work.

Start with the three key considerations every good home office covers—efficiency, comfort, and separation. **Efficiency** ensures you get your work done as quickly and easily as possible. **Comfort** combines ergonomic features and fixtures that make the physical workspace not only tolerable, but pleasant throughout the workday. **Separation** is one of the biggest issues in setting up a home office. It means developing a space that doesn't interfere with other activities in the home and vice

Home office spacing has to balance accessibility and unrestricted movement. In this relatively small whole-room workspace, the placement of the desk allows for comfortable movement behind it and plenty of room in front for visitors and meetings.

As this highly efficient and quite handsome office proves, a backyard utility space can provide an excellent place for your home office.

versa, so that you can effectively step away from the home office when your workday comes to an end. Get it right and you'll still enjoy your home as a place you can comfortably live, socialize, relax, and even forget about work. Separation is also important in other ways. If your workspace is too integrated into the home, then noise, family members' activities, and even pets may intrude on the workspace and your productivity time.

Correctly integrating any home office is more complicated than it might first appear. Beyond the obvious concerns of the proper equipment, a place to sit, and the right amount of storage for whatever you use and create in the process of what you do, there are a lot other considerations, which we'll cover in this book.

First things first, though. You'll start by figuring out the perfect landing spot for your new work area. Once you've chosen that spot, you'll develop the the layout and choose the furniture and equipment that will make your work possible. You'll deal with extending any necessary services to the workspace and getting your technology up and running. Finally, you'll work on getting the look and feel of the space just right, so that it is a pleasing place in which to spend long hours making a living.

This can all seem a little overwhelming. Don't worry. This book has your back. Start by taking a breath and turning the page, because the rest of this book will lead you step by step through the process. Save yourself some time by making notes as you read, or just mark pages that apply to your particular work situation. Follow the process laid out in these chapters, and one thing's for sure: creating your home office will be as enjoyable as it is rewarding.

# HOME OFFICE INSPIRATION GALLERY

From small to large, technologically advanced to basic, and private to busy, home offices aren't one size fits all. In the rest of the book, you'll learn how to think about your particular home office needs and make the best decisions for your design. But start here and return for inspiration and ideas as needed.

Thoughtfully picking furniture, such as the black chairs in this home office that match the paint and décor of the room, is one key way to ensure the home office doesn't stick out like a sore thumb.

Positioning is everything in a home office. Here, the computer monitor is placed so that the large window exposure doesn't create glare on the screen. Gauzy curtains diffuse the light so there are no hot spots in the worker's field of view.

Personalizing a home office is a way to make yourself more comfortable at work and is one of the big benefits of a home-based workspace. The key is striking a balance between inspiring and distracting.

When choosing a location for your home office, keep in mind that easy access to outdoor areas is a fantastic feature and a great way to refresh and refocus with regular fresh-air breaks.

A well-appointed home office in a modern backyard shed makes best use of the available space and utilities, including a relaxed meeting area for interacting with clients and colleagues and a dedicated workspace with the desk as a centerpiece. The style is streamlined, organized, and visually appealing.

Small, awkward rooms or spaces in the home can be ideal for a home office because they may not be suitable for any other purpose and are often out of the main traffic flow of the home.

If clients are an integral part of your work, your home office design will need to walk a line between informal and formal, between comfort and image. The balance is maintained in this small whole-room workspace.

In space-challenged homes, you may need to be creative and flexible in your search for office space. Under-stair areas are often worth exploiting. If you can minimize your working environment and storage needs, this can be the perfect location for a compact home workspace.

Wireless technology allows for clean, streamlined home office setups like this one. Professionals can work on laptops that go with them on the road and easily connect to the printer when at home—without a tangle of cords.

An adjustable task light is indispensible in a home office that is carved out of a larger space because the vast majority of larger spaces aren't sufficiently lit for focused desk work. An extendable-arm desk lamp serves the purpose handily.

A kitchen alcove such as this one can be an excellent landing spot for a home office, as long as your business can handle the hustle and bustle of an active area of the house.

The best way to integrate a home office into a guest bedroom is to replace the bed with a sleeper sofa, as has been done here.

Small, out-of-the-way spaces are natural choices for home offices because the office won't disrupt traffic flow through the larger room—and vice versa.

Attics are some of the best locations for home offices and work that requires focus, quiet, and concentration. The attic-based office is a great way to ensure work stays "at" work and home life stays home.

One of the wonderful things about taking over an entire room for a home office is that it allows the home-based professional to design a stunning space that does not necessarily need to be tied to, or blended with, the home's interior design.

# CHAPTER 1

# CHOOSING A LOCATION FOR YOUR HOME OFFICE

Just as with real estate, location is everything in creating your ideal home office. Put your workspace in the wrong place and you'll detract from the look, feel, and enjoyment of the overall home. Just as bad, the wrong landing space will make your work harder to do rather than easier. Start with a simple stroll through the house. Look at the space from a work perspective—specifically, through the lens of what you do for a living. The best potential sites for your home office are sure to jump out at you. As you consider different sites, ask yourself the questions on the following pages. The answers will lead you to just the right location for your job and the way you work.

For people who don't have the space to dedicate an entire room to a home office, a good location may be within a larger living or family room, like this unobtrusive example. You have to consider your specific work needs to decide if such a placement will work for you.

# THINGS TO CONSIDER

Here is the at-a-glance list of the questions you need to ask yourself at the very beginning of your home office planning journey. We'll examine each one in more detail in the following pages to get you thinking, and each topic is covered more extensively throughout the course of the book.

- How much space will you need?
- How will the traffic flow work?
- What will be the visual impact?
- Will you be comfortable in the area for hours on end?
- Is it quiet?
- Do you need space for visitors?
- Are the services where you need them to be?
- Does the space need to serve multiple purposes?

### How much space will you need?

Let's face it: try though you might, you will never fit 10 pounds into a 5-pound bag. You'll need to look at your potential spaces with common sense. If you're a draftsman who requires both a small work desk and a larger drafting table, the limited and narrow dead space at the end of a hallway is not going to cut it as a workspace. Most types of work, however, are fairly adaptable to available space. Visualize your work and the tasks you do to determine the amount of space you'll need.

The size of a desktop can be a matter of preference. A 5-foot-wide work surface is the norm in office buildings, but you may be able to comfortably fit your work onto a much smaller desktop. Compare these two workers: one doesn't work long hours and can stay contained to a small table end with her laptop; the other needs to spread out many papers and tools for her work.

### How will the traffic flow work?

Think about the ways in which other people in the house—including guests—interact with the space. What about pets? Will traffic flow represent a disruption, or is it a non-issue for you? Before dedicating a space to your office, you may want to test the traffic flow in that space for a couple of days while working from a laptop. If the traffic in and out of the area proves distracting, look for ways to reduce the movement through that area or mark that space as less than ideal and test another area.

### What will be the visual impact?

Do it right, and the home office will blend with your home's interior design or even add to the look you've established. However, in certain places—especially where the home office must be integrated into an existing room—there is a risk that the workspace will stick out like a sore thumb. A poorly thought-out home office can flat-out ruin the look and feel of a room. That risk is even greater in smaller, more cluttered rooms.

This simple and compact home office is placed in a corner of the living room out of necessity, but it is still out of the way of traffic flow and takes advantage of the natural light and pleasant color scheme of the existing room.

## Will you be comfortable in the area for hours on end?

This is a hard question to answer, but it is important to think about. Is the space you're considering using for a home office a space you unconsciously avoid? Can you easily change whatever it is you might not like about the room? Are you easily distracted, and will the view from the home office or proximity to other activities, such as kids playing, disrupt your work process?

## Is it quiet?

Noise isn't just a matter of your own comfort and concentration, it's also about the professionalism you project. A dog barking constantly in the background, or the sound of a washer and dryer running, isn't going to project a polished image on a phone call or videoconference. See more info on soundproofing on page 37.

If your work requires quiet focus and little interaction with clients or colleagues, an isolated alcove such as this may be the ideal, quiet, out-of-the-way spot for your home office.

This room is set up not only for utility, but also to create a welcoming environment for the many clients that visit. Visitors have ample room to spread out when sitting in the comfortable, modern chairs.

## Do you need space for visitors?

What type of visitor will you have—colleagues, clients, consultants, or vendors? This will determine not only how much extra space you need, but also how formal the space needs to be. You want to make any guests comfortable and create the illusion of a dedicated workspace rather than an overly casual home environment. Even if your business is fairly informal, you'll want a clean, well-lit, and comfortable space to meet with clients. In general, any work that requires regular meetings with individuals who may be responsible for writing you a check calls for a dedicated space. If your work requires collaborating with colleagues, the bar for accommodating those individuals is not as high as it is for clients. Working with colleagues

at a dining room table may suit your purposes just fine. However, you may need to add certain equipment to your home office, like a large brainstorming table or whiteboard.

## Are the services where you need them to be?

If you've lived in your space for any period of time, there is no doubt you quickly learned its technology hot spots and dead zones. A few tech essentials (see page 68) can help boost the reach of your Wi-Fi or make the most of fewer outlets, but when setting up a permanent home office, now is the time to consider investing in other ways of getting services you need where you need them (see page 50).

### Does the space need to serve multiple purposes?

If you will need to use the space in which your home office is located during off-hours for family activities, socializing, or even just your own down time, you need to take those uses into consideration. A divider that screens off a work area, or a setup where all work materials can be concealed on nights and weekends, is ideal for home offices placed in large rooms, like a living room or kitchen, or in the corner of a master bedroom. Where the work area is part of a guest bedroom, the space should still look welcoming and the work furniture should blend with the other furnishings to create an eye-pleasing sense of calm.

When your home office also serves as a guest bedroom, improve your visitor's stay by keeping the business side of the room largely hidden. This office balances homey touches with office essentials in pleasing way.

# HOME OFFICE ROOM OPTIONS

In theory, a home office can be set up in any room in the house. In practice, there is usually one room that is the most natural landing spot. Finding the perfect location is about balancing the space available in any room, how much (and how) it's used by other family members, and the particulars of the work you do. There are six general options, each of which we'll explore further in the remainder of this chapter. You can place your office within an existing room that already has another function; you can convert a closet into an office; you can utilize a transition space instead of a room; you can dedicate an entire room to your office; you can renovate a utility space; or you can use an outbuilding to house your office.

## Existing Rooms

Carving a workspace out of an existing room is one of the most common ways to create a home office. In fact, many people have already done this to one degree or another in order to have a dedicated work area for paperwork and tasks such as paying bills. However, if you're going to spend eight to ten hours a day there, you have to be more intentional and thoughtful about how you achieve a balance and a pleasant shared space.

This nook at the rear of a spare room provides a good space for someone with minimal work needs. Ample curtains and blinds ensure that the lighting is controllable.

Kitchen-based home offices work best for professionals who don't need full-service offices. Someone like a real estate agent or salesperson—who can regularly count on being out of the office—will find the space appealing. This home workspace is kept out of the main traffic flow of kitchen business.

## Kitchen

Kitchens are utilitarian spaces; unless yours is the lucky exception, most kitchens are pushed for space. That means that kitchen-based home offices inevitably must be compact and limited. These are options for individuals whose work life is mostly digital and who don't need abundant storage, or professionals such as real estate agents who will be away from the office for a good deal of their workday. The upside to a kitchen workspace is that you can take over nearby cabinets for hidden storage that blends seamlessly with the rest of the room.

The challenge of integrating a home office into a kitchen can be summed up in one word: blending. Because kitchens have so many surfaces, finishes, and appliances, the look is already busy. Adding a contrasting workspace isn't a good idea and will tend to look jarring. Plan on concealing storage and using innovative cabinet features such as pullout shelves to hide electronics, files, and supplies. When looking at a kitchen as a home for your home office, consider the following options.

**Nook it.** Alcoves and nooks are natural home office spaces because they are out of the main traffic flow of what is usually the most hectic room in the house. You'll still need to visually complement the rest of the room, but separation is easier to maintain. This is essential in busy kitchens where you may need to work while someone else is cooking dinner, for example.

**Go vertical.** Ideally, whatever space you choose has unused wall area on which you can hang a corkboard, whiteboard, or magnetic strip for putting up important reminders, notes, sketches, or ideas. If you're placing the home office under a kitchen window, you'll need to plan where things you'd normally hang will go. Keep in mind that you may need to assert to the family that the board is for your work use only—if members of the family try to co-opt your board for to-do lists and family calendars, you may need to place a new, separate board for family use somewhere else the kitchen.

**Containerize.** Space is at a premium in most kitchens. A great way to make use of whatever space is available without detracting from the kitchen's design is to store office supplies and general work items in containers. Decorative bins or boxes that match the kitchen's color scheme are ideal to accommodate the range of materials you might need to keep on hand for your work, from paper supplies to coiled computer cords.

Family members (furry or otherwise) will have easy access to a kitchen workspace, so if you don't mind the distractions, a kitchen workspace could work for you.

A dedicated board on the wall in front of your workspace can maximize the utility of a small area.

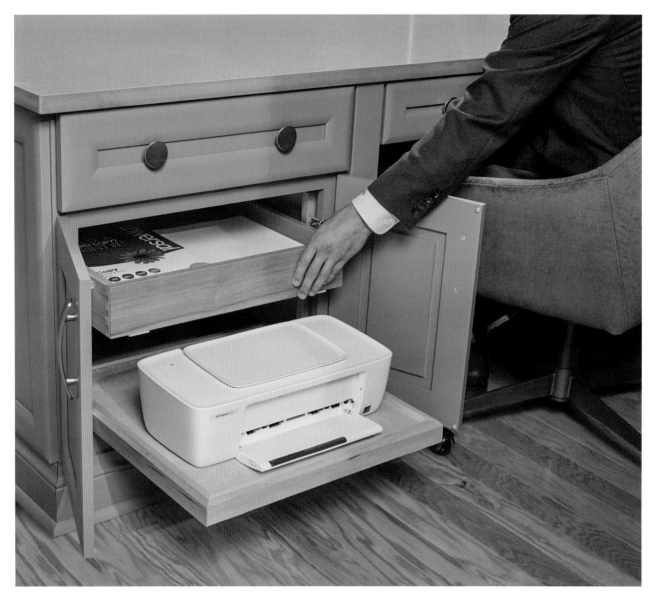

Cabinet manufacturers have developed many nifty options for the home office worker, such as this one with a pullout printer shelf and a supplies tray to hold paper and printer supplies. It's even designed with a hidden outlet for the power cord.

**Retrofit.** Chances are that regardless of what your job is, you'll likely need to co-opt nearby kitchen cabinets for storage. Unfortunately, kitchen cabinets are not designed to store office supplies and equipment that should be kept out of sight. Take heart; it's easy to change up the interior of most kitchen cabinets with the range of aftermarket add-ons available through suppliers nationwide. From slide-out printer shelves to hinged under-counter keyboard trays to pocketed drawer inserts, you can usually find exactly what you need to customize the cabinets for the type of work you do.

This living room home office is well integrated into the room, with matching storage space and a monitor that echoes the look of the wall-mounted flat-screen TV. The design of the office means that it blends in with the surroundings so that the space is comfortable and pleasant during non-work hours. Obviously, work hours wil be limited to periods when no one is relaxing in front of the TV.

## Living rooms and family rooms

The challenge of integrating a home office into a common shared space is keeping work out of the room's traffic flow and busiest areas. There are a number of reasons for this. Kids and pets can easily scatter work documents and other essentials without meaning to, and, ideally, the space should be usable even when you're finished working. If you're considering a living room or family room as a potential office site, think about your hours. Do you work late? Chances are, if you do, activity in even a large living space is going to intrude on your work focus. This is especially true of TV watching; it's difficult to do any work

with a TV at volume a few steps away from your desk. (This won't be an issue if you live alone, of course.) Also consider how you socialize in the room. Will it seem odd to have people over for drinks or a game night with a desk and work materials in the room?

When you've settled on a living room, family room, or den for your home office, look for dead zones—awkward areas of the room that see little use. Living room corners are especially good locations for an L-shaped desk that can nest into the floor space without having much of an impact on the overall look and use of the room.

A bedroom is a good location for a modest home office, one that doesn't require a great deal of storage or extra technology.

## Bedrooms

A bedroom, especially a guest bedroom, can be a great place for a home office. Integrating a workspace, however, can require a bit of adaptation. Start with the lighting. Many guest bedrooms are lit by a single overhead fixture that likely won't provide adequate illumination for a full-time home office. That means you'll need to supplement with task lighting suitable to whatever work you do. The power for this lighting—and for the computer and electronic equipment you need to do your job—can be another challenge. Second and third bedrooms in older homes often have few outlets and may have no phone jacks. If your business requires a lot of computer equipment or other electronics (such as a graphic designer working with multiple monitors and a powerful computer), all hooked up to an "uninterrupted power supply" unit, you may need to upgrade the electrical service in the room; otherwise, you risk overloading the circuit. In most cases, you'll at least be faced with running an extension cord or placing the office to take advantage of existing services in the room.

Covering a daybed with pillows is a great way to convert a guest bedroom workspace into an informal home office that doesn't really look like it was tacked onto a bedroom. Notice how the whimsical style of this room is carried through in the choice of desk and decorations for the work area. Those choices create a design continuity that makes the room pleasant regardless of what it's being used for.

# Closets

The right closet can be a surprisingly wonderful landing space for a home office. Although we tend to think of them as one space, closets vary in size and layout—from the roomy expanses of a master bedroom walk-in closet, to the functional, utilitarian nature of a guest-bedroom closet, to the more unusual potential offered in a hallway linen closet or an older pantry closet right off a kitchen. Every one of them can be successfully converted into an efficient office, as long as you and your work can adapt to the limitations of the unusual physical environment.

A key benefit to just about any closet is definitive separation. Leave the door or doors on the closet when you convert it and, at the end of the workday, simply close the doors to put the office—and your work—out of sight and out of mind. Add a lock and the office will enjoy a measure of security. This also means that for a closet in a bedroom, the workspace won't visually intrude on the overall room's design and function during off-hours and down time. That's essential if you're going to fully relax in your master bedroom.

Placing a home office in a closet does not mean creating a drab workspace. The designer who works in this office has it outfitted so that everything she needs is close at hand. There is storage aplenty, and with the chair pushed in, the mirrored closet doors can be securely closed.

Once you've identified a specific closet that will be suitable for a workspace, it's time to roll up your sleeves and turn it into a productive home base from which to earn your living.

**Start with what's already there.** The standard closet in a basic second bedroom has a long shelf above a hanging bar. Less often, it will have basic side shelves or a divider with multiple hanging bars at different heights. In most circumstances, it's relatively easy—and preferable—to remove the existing closet storage structures. Yes, you will probably need shelves and could potentially reuse what is there. But any shelves in a closet home office need to be at precisely the heights and locations for the work you do, the equipment you own, and what you need to store. The closet space should accommodate your home office, not the other way around.

With the closet stripped bare, **take precise measurements.** This will be key to seamlessly fitting in a work surface and exactly the storage features you want and need, where you need them. Make a note of the interior depth, width, and height. Use a stud finder to identify stud locations on side walls and the back wall. You'll need to know this when you start installing wall-mounted units.

This fully equipped and customized closet office is an example of how much can fit into an astutely designed space. Basic floating U shelves match the installed desk. The spacious desk includes plenty of room for a printer, fax machine, and work area.

Next, think about how you **envision working in the space.** Would it make sense to have lots of small hanging storage features like wire baskets on pegboard? Do you want a tower of cubbies along one side to hold many small items, or would you be better served with a sturdy central shelf supporting a collection of magazine file holders or simple storage boxes? Do you need open wall space for a large corkboard or whiteboard? Include all these elements in a rough scale sketch of the closet.

**Downsize the desk surface.** Unless you're converting a walk-in or pantry closet, you'll be working with a limited depth in which to place a desk. That means most traditional desks won't fit in the closet. The legs of standalone desks also tend to take up a lot of precious floor space in a closet office. That's why the best desk is a floating desk—one attached to the back and side walls. You can create your own floating desk with very little DIY expertise; see the sidebar below for instructions.

**Add storage.** With the desk in place, you can now add the storage you'll need. Use open storage—specifically shelving—to avoid making the office feel overly claustrophobic. You can add floating shelves or you can nest cubby boxes or cabinets along one side of the closet or the other. It's best to screw everything into wall studs. When placing shelves, make sure anything you will be putting on your desk—especially your computer monitor—will have sufficient clearance below the shelf.

## DIY Floating Desk

**1.** Take precise measurements for desk depth and width, and check them twice.

**2.** Measure and mark multiple points 28 inches (71cm) up from the floor on the side walls and the back wall of the closet. Use a level to draw straight horizontal lines from mark to mark.

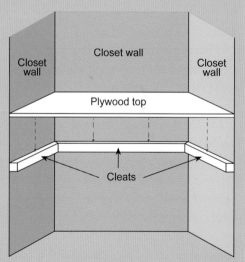

**3.** Head to your local home improvement store. Pick out a ¾-inch (2cm) or 1-inch (2.5cm) plywood—a hardwood like birch plywood if you want to stain or finish the desk naturally, or a less expensive softwood (also sold as "sheathing") plywood if you're going to paint the desk. Ask the store associates to cut the plywood to the dimensions you measured in step 1, and to cut four 1 inch x 2 inch (2.5 x 5cm) pine cleats, 12 inches (30cm) long. Buy a small tin of wood putty and a putty knife; also buy paint and a brush if you are painting your desk, or your finish of choice if you're not.

**4.** Screw the cleats to the walls. Use two on the back wall and one on each side wall, centering the cleats and lining the top edges up with the lines you drew with the level. Screw the cleats into wall studs using 2-inch (5cm) deck screws, or screws and anchors.

**5.** Paint the cleats to match the wall. Paint or finish the plywood with at least two coats—top, bottom, and edges. If you're painting the plywood, coat the edge that will face out with wood putty, sand it, and then paint it. When the desktop is dry, position it on top of the cleats, and you're ready to go!

**Paint for productivity.** Choose paint colors and finishes for your closet home office carefully—they will have an outsize influence on the feel, mood, and comfort of the work environment. Lighter and brighter colors are generally more pleasing and conducive to work over the long term; muddy, dark, or washed-out hues will tend to drag down the energy level of the space. The surface finish is almost as important as the color itself. Although you might be tempted to use a gloss or semi-gloss sheen to bounce light around in the space, avoid that temptation. Those finishes can create hot spots and glare that will be distracting while you work. Also avoid flat or matte finishes, which can appear dirty and timeworn in short order and will minimize light in the space—stick to satin or eggshell finishes.

**Electrify within reason.** If the closet has wired internal lighting, it may involve a modest expense to have an electrician install an electrical outlet inside the closet on the same circuit as the lighting. However, in most cases, workaround solutions are going to be much more palatable. The vast majority of closet home offices are best served with a power strip run into the closet from the nearest outlet. The cord for the strip can be secured along baseboard or cove molding with nail-in or adhesive cable clips. Make sure you supplement the lighting as needed to ensure a comfortable work environment.

This homeowner found a perfect home office space in an underused pantry off the kitchen. Don't be afraid to look outside the box—and in any available closet—to find a workspace that might suit you.

**Exploit the vertical** in a closet office by using vertical hangers like magazine racks, hooks, magnetic strips, and hanging bars where applicable for what you need to store. Of course, a wall surface can also be useful for bulletin boards to keep something like a to-do list front and center in your field of view and top of mind. You can even use chalkboard paint to paint a square on the wall right over your desk so that you can quickly write and erase messages to yourself.

A closet office can be concealable and stylish at the same time. When not in use, this closet hides behind lacquered bi-fold doors and the chair rolls away to another part of the apartment.

## The Case Against Shared Computers

Considering having your home computer do double duty as your home office unit? Think again. There are lots of good reasons to use a separate computer dedicated to your work. Here are the top three.

**Security.** Viruses can be a frustrating nuisance on a home computer, but at work, they can be a pure income-killer, putting valuable data in peril. It goes without saying that you should install security software on any computer you use to make a living. But you can't account for what a bored child might download or click on. It may also be the case that you work with sensitive files and client data. Best standards and practices are to minimize users on the computer in that instance.

**Convenience.** Inevitably in a busy household, schedules are going to clash. You might need to finish up your work while your child needs to finish his or her homework before going to bed. Maybe your partner wants to videoconference with friends or relatives on the opposite coast at the same time you need to check a report from a colleague. A separate work computer alleviates all that. It also means that you don't have to sift through file after file of family photos to find the image of the house you need to send to a real estate client.

**Tax benefits.** The clearer the separation between home and office, the less likely it is that you'll be audited or encounter issues when taking tax deductions for a home office. See Tax Advantages on page 119 for more info.

# Transitional Spaces

It can seem counterintuitive, but the perfect home office space may be lurking where you least expect. The longer we live in a house, the more our eye learns to visually ignore any part of the house we simply pass through. Seen or not, those odd areas may represent usable square footage. These "transition" spaces have limitations; the most obvious is roominess. Any of them will only accommodate a small work surface and a modest office setup. Working in a transition space is going to be most comfortable when you're able to "micronize" everything—using a laptop rather than a desktop computer, digitizing as much paperwork as possible, and working on documents on the computer instead of in paper form. This type of home office may also require that you use Bluetooth peripherals so that you can, for instance, keep a printer in another room. However, if the work you do doesn't require that you spread out much and you're comfortable adapting to the limited area, you can quite possibly have a home office that makes minimal, if any, impact on your home's interior design.

All that said, a transition space must fulfill some basic requirements. If you work full time at home, it's important to be exposed to some amount of natural light. If you park your business control center in a dark hallway, you'll be pretty grumpy and uncomfortable by the end of the workday. You'll also need access to an electrical outlet even if your equipment is minimal. Other considerations are specific to the particular transition space.

The easiest way to incorporate an office under the stairs is if the stairs are an "open" construction, so that the under-stair area is not enclosed. With some effort and thoughtfulness, you can make a wonderful workspace under just about any set of stairs.

### Under-stair areas

If your home has stairs, the area underneath may be ripe for exploiting. Even if there are already built-in units in the location, it's easy enough to remove them (being careful not to undermine the supporting structure of the stairs, or bringing in a qualified contractor to do the work for you) and set up an office in the cavity. The trick with under-stair alcoves, as with other transition spaces, is getting power to the area. Obviously, it probably won't work to run an extension cord from a nearby outlet. That means you may have to plan on the cost of having an electrician run a circuit to the space. Do that, though, and you'll have a tidy home office with the opportunity to custom build exactly the professional storage you need. You'll also have a workspace out of the flow of traffic in the house, and one that exploits square footage that might well otherwise have gone unused.

## Halls

You walk down them every day. You rarely think about them, and you take them for granted. Still, the alcove space at the end of a long hall, or a dogleg in a wider passageway, can be all the square footage you need to create a useful, efficient, and even quiet home office. Getting power to your equipment may be the deal-breaker, though, because older homes rarely feature electrical outlets in hallways. You'll also need to make sure that the chair won't be in the way of the natural traffic flow through the house.

## Entry areas

Perhaps you're lucky enough to have a large entry foyer. More likely, you have a mudroom that seems to collect clothing and other cast-offs in equal measure. This type of room can sometimes be outfitted with a desk and office setup if you think through how the space is used and how you want to work. Honestly, this is not the first option on most home workers' lists and will probably only suit you if your particular entry area is larger and has a good amount of dead space to work with. The one big advantage to an office in a space like this is that at the end of the day, you truly leave work behind as you enter the home proper.

The end of this wide hall was isolated just enough to serve as an ideal home office location. The abundant storage surrounding the desk might look custom, but the entire handsome structure was purchased from a cabinet manufacturer. This type of turnkey option can be a great go-to resource for the homeowner looking to place a home office in an unusual location.

# Full-Room Home Offices

Taking over an entire room of the house for your home office can seem a little indulgent, but keep in mind that you will quite possibly spend more time in that office space than you will watching TV in the living room or even sleeping in your bedroom. It also becomes much easier to calculate a home office tax deduction. Where you have the extra room to spare, a full-room home office can be a boon to productivity and make for a much more comfortable working environment. A dedicated room may even be a necessity if you work with sensitive materials and need to keep them and your computer equipment extra secure from prying eyes or theft. This option is also ideal for anyone who needs to entertain clients or accommodate colleagues on a regular basis. A work-at-home lawyer, bookkeeper, or salesperson might all benefit from a full-room office.

The most likely rooms for a dedicated office are a small guest bedroom, a bonus room, a relatively unused family room, or a den. Ideally, a standalone home office should have a door. That's not just a matter of security; being able to physically close off your workspace when you're done for the day will help you avoid burnout, depression, and the overwork that is common with home offices.

Not all home offices are computer-centric. This seamstress, for example, needs racks for hanging works-in-progress, plenty of table space for pinning and cutting fabric, and storage shelves for supplies. A full-room home office is essential for her.

# Soundproofing

Simple soundproofing options can help make a workspace tolerable and avoid bothering family members when you have to work late or have early video meetings. You don't need a recording studio setup to enjoy a fairly quiet workspace—even in a busy, noisy household. Choose an option (or combination of options) that works for you.

**Install sound-deadening panels.** These are surprisingly effective at deadening sounds, especially in rooms with hard surfaces such as wood floors and metal filing cabinets. Sound-deadening surfaces can be as simple as a thick, plush rug, an upholstered screen or divider, or even a wall-hung tapestry. You can also buy special sound-deadening art and decorative panels meant to absorb sound waves.

**Swap for a solid-core door.** Is the door to your home office hollow? Then it's not blocking sound effectively and is a weak spot in your soundproofing. Replace it with a solid-core door. Alternatively, hang a soundproof door blanket over it.

**Caulk cracks.** If there are any crevices or holes in drywall near ducts, utility boxes, or other entry-and-exit points in the room, noise could sneak in. Seal them up.

Simple soundproofing panels come in a range of sizes, shapes, and colors. Many are artistic, like the hexagons shown here, and most can be used as a partial surface that offers a degree of sound-deadening without the expense or effort of covering every wall in the space.

**Add a fresh layer of paint.** Believe it or not, soundproofing paint exists, and it can reduce noise by up to 30 percent. If you're customizing a room for a home office, it's a great opportunity to choose a new color and soundproof at the same time.

**Hang sound-blocking curtains.** If the noise coming from outside is a problem, try hanging special sound-blocking curtains. You'll have to sacrifice some natural light, but you can counteract that by strategically adding artificial lighting.

**Mask sound locally.** To tune out normal household noise to focus on work, try a white noise machine, which can mask irritating noises, including nearby construction and the everyday sounds from adjacent apartments. Noise-canceling headphones can be another great way to achieve relative silence.

**Professional solutions.** If household noise might disrupt your business or if the noise produced by your work might disrupt the household, more involved options may be called for. These could include lining a wall or walls with sound-silencer panels, installing acoustic sound-deadening ceiling tiles, and adding specialized door-seal kits. These are all expensive and more labor-intensive options, so consult with an acoustic professional.

## Utility Spaces

Garages, basements, enclosed porches, and attics all represent excellent potential locations for a home office. In most cases, though, exploiting that promise will involve some structural work. Specifically, you'll have to ensure that the area is properly heated and cooled and that there is adequate air circulation to ensure comfort throughout the workday. You may also have to upgrade electrical service to the space in order to meet the needs of your equipment and guarantee that the lighting is conducive to being productive. And don't forget safety—exposed, shedding insulation or flimsy floorboards are not safe elements in any workspace.

Getting your converted room up to snuff can be costly and time consuming, so make sure you really need this to be your solution. Standalone or expansive home office spaces are most useful for jobs that can't necessarily be streamlined. A self-employed graphic designer, for instance, may need a suite of expensive and space-consuming technology, different work areas in the office for different tasks, and an abundant amount of physical storage for printouts and other materials. That all points to a dedicated home office space with plenty of square footage.

Even after you've decided on one of these spaces for your home office, you have to keep another consideration in mind: how the conversion will impact the home value. No home office is successful if it adversely affects the potential resale value of your home. Make sure your converted room will add to the value, not detract from it. Ensuring positive value is a good argument for hiring a contractor. If you choose to use one, do your research, make sure your contractor is licensed and insured and has had experience doing conversions similar to what you want, and get everything in writing.

Take heart, though: improving an unfinished attic or a rough basement for a home office means you may be able to convert that space into a living area later on. That means it's a home upgrade, and some of the costs of improvements may be tax deductible (see Tax Advantages on page 119).

Even if you don't have to undergo a complete renovation, upgrading just surfaces and finishes will create the polished appearance of a professional office. That's more than a superficial consideration—adding the visual indicators of a work environment will improve your mental outlook and your approach to your work.

With the right features, like sufficient ventilation, adequate lighting, and enough headroom, an attic like this one can become a viable workspace.

A converted attic can make a comfortable, quiet home office space far out of the rough and tumble of busier areas in the house. An attic home office also offers a lot of potential security if you work with sensitive materials.

## Attic offices

The first step in converting attic space into a home office is making a sober assessment of the potential floor plan and existing characteristics of the attic and deciding if it can be turned into a comfortable workspace with a minimum of expense, time, and effort.

Start by monitoring the daytime temperature in the attic. Heat concentrates in most attics, which can be a real problem from early summer through fall. You may be able to install fans or air conditioning, but attics with no windows or only one small window are usually not good potential home office spaces.

One very important consideration is headroom. You have to be able to move around without constantly ducking to avoid a sloping ceiling or rafters. Limited attic headroom is usually remedied by installing one or more dormers—a major construction project not suited to a do-it-yourself approach.

Any attic space that might serve as a home office will also need to offer conveniently placed electrical outlets and enough available wattage on the circuit to support your computer, equipment, and office lighting. Having an electrician upgrade the circuit and install outlets and switches usually won't break the bank, but it is a significant enough investment to factor into the decision of whether the attic is the best place to put the office.

Available light is another crucial consideration; read more about lighting in general on page 87. For an attic office specifically, you may be able to strategically place mirrors to bounce the available natural light around. You could also add a solar tube, a small skylight tube equipped with a dispersing lens that spreads the incoming light throughout the room. This can be installed in a roof at a fraction of the cost a skylight would entail and can even be a project for an experienced DIYer.

## Basement offices

Just as the very top of the house offers excellent potential, so does the very bottom. However, be careful not to jam a square peg into a round hole. One big stumbling block to basement offices can be water infiltration and dampness or mold issues. The last thing you want for your job-related paperwork is for it to be constantly moist. High humidity is also far from ideal for computers and related equipment like printers. If you have ongoing moisture problems in your basement, it's probably best to cross it off your list of potential home office locations.

If your basement is watertight, completely or mostly underground, and especially if it is finished, it can be an ideal site for a quiet and comfortable home office. Basements, like attics, are isolated from the busiest areas of the home and consequently lend themselves to concentration and focus on work. It's usually also an easy improvement to run electrical outlets if needed. Completely below-ground basements maintain relatively stable year-round temperatures, making them comfortable throughout the day.

The drawback to even a finished belowground basement is the lack of natural light. For some people, that's just not an acceptable tradeoff. Because the lack of natural light can have a strong impact on mood and mental state, carefully consider the lighting situation in your basement. You can augment a basement home office with SAD lights (see page 90), which will offset the lack of natural illumination to some degree, but nothing replaces direct sunlight.

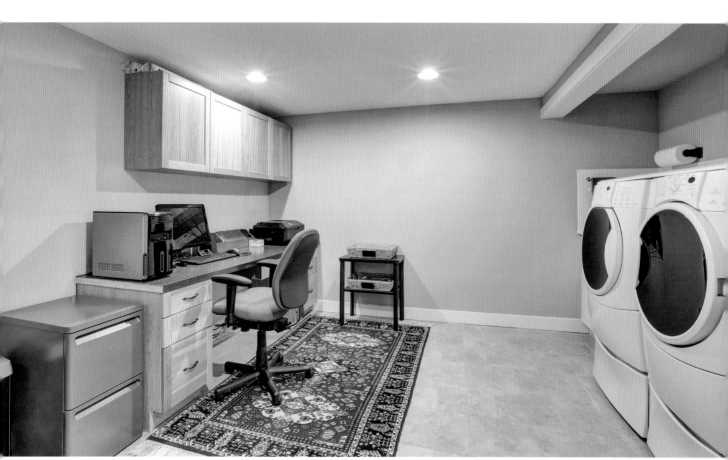

This functional home office in a finished basement's laundry area is comfortable and well-lit by warm, cheery recessed halogen lights that keep the office from feeling cold or sterile.

Want to have the best of both worlds with your garage office? Open up one half as a carport and leave one bay enclosed. The garage door here was replaced with rustic barn doors and the detached garage was updated with new siding and insulation.

## Garage offices

If your home is equipped with a room for your cars, it's worth considering turning all or part of that into an office. After all, which is more important—a spacious place to earn a living in comfort, or a comfortable indoor parking spot for the family sedan?

The best of both worlds is a two-bay garage with enough space to convert one bay into an office, while leaving the other for your car. In any case, attached garages are the best option because they offer close proximity to the house. Depending on how many walls the garage shares with the home, the unfinished space may stay relatively comfortable throughout the seasons, requiring only a space heater and a good fan.

You'll want to upgrade your garage space to one degree or another to make it look and feel more like an indoor home office. How far you go depends on how polished you need the space to be and what your available budget is.

Start with the walls. Insulating and hanging drywall in the garage is a fairly inexpensive improvement and one

that doesn't require much skill or expertise, can be done over a weekend, and changes the look and feel of any garage almost instantaneously.

Next comes the floor. Concrete is rarely a comfortable surface for any home office. Fortunately, a number of manufacturers make easy-to-use, click-to-install garage floor tiles. Most of these are soft-surface products that are easy on feet over time.

The garage door is usually the biggest issue in converting a garage space into a home office. In almost all cases, you'll need to add weatherstripping around the edges of the door, and a sweep, rubber block, or other weatherstripping to the bottom of the door. If your garage door is showing its age, this may be the perfect opportunity to replace it.

Finally, be ready to adapt the lighting scheme to the space. The existing overhead lights probably won't cut it. See more about lighting on page 87.

## Porch offices

The right enclosed porch might be a suitable landing spot for your home office. A porch is usually only a realistic candidate if it is enclosed with windows rather than screens and the local climate doesn't experience temperature extremes. On the plus side, a porch can offer a home office with unrivaled views and a way to leave and enter the office without disturbing the rest of the household.

Most porches do not have electrical service, so that will be the single biggest change you'll have to make to move a home office into the space. Fortunately, there are companies out there that offer all-in-one services to enclose porches, making them three- or four-season rooms with all the electricity you need.

If you opt to adapt a porch for your home office, take steps to secure your equipment, because most porches are exposed and easily accessible from the outside. You'll also want to consider carefully where you position your desk and computer monitor, because you'll likely receive strong natural light from different directions during the day.

An enclosed porch can offer stunning vistas for a home office. This rooftop home office with outdoor deck access embodies the same principles of making the most of views and creating a finished space from an unconventional—normally exterior—area.

This underused back porch could become a home office. If the climate isn't too hot or cold, the large glass windows and door can be a boon, especially if regulated by hanging curtains for light control and privacy.

# Outbuildings

A completely separate office in your backyard isn't the solution for everyone working from home, but it can be an excellent choice for the right work situation and for the sole proprietor. Because these types of home offices require such a significant commitment and financial investment, they are best for full-fledged small businesses that may require additional employees in the future, or work that involves a stream of clients who expect an official residence for the business. You also need a fairly large yard to accommodate an outbuilding if it isn't already built. This can be an especially wonderful option for someone who wants a home office completely separate from the home and isn't afraid to dive into a big DIY project.

The three ways to have a completely separate home office away from home are to build a new structure, convert an existing shed or outbuilding, or buy a prefab unit. For most people, the last one will be most preferable because it's a turnkey solution that can be put in place quickly and with little effort on the homeowner's part. It is, however, often the most expensive way to go.

In any case, there are key concerns common to any separate structure. Start with local zoning and housing association rules, which may prohibit or significantly limit separate-structure workspaces. Even if they don't, local building codes will mandate important considerations such as lot-line setbacks (how close a new building can be to a border of the property) and how and where you can run plumbing and electrical services to an outbuilding.

A handsome prefab shed like this one can be a turnkey option for a well-outfitted office that is far enough removed from the house to avoid all distractions.

### Existing shed or outbuilding

Start by judging the condition of the structure. Ask yourself the following questions:

- Is it structurally sound?
- Is it weatherproof? If not, what will it take to seal the building from the elements?
- Are there windows? (Natural light is crucial to happiness at work.)
- Does the structure have existing services (electrical and/or plumbing)? If not, can they easily be run to it?
- Will the available square footage accommodate your work furniture and equipment, with room to spare?
- Is the structure suitable to receive clients or visitors if your business requires those interactions?
- What will modifying the structure cost and how long will it take (relative to when you need the space)?

Don't be put off by bare studs and a plywood floor. Even if you have a small shed that you normally use to house yard tools, it can probably be converted into a cozy home office with less effort than you might think. Even cutting an opening and installing a window isn't that difficult. Shallow wall cavities can be insulated with products like thin board insulation. As long as the space is comfortable, you don't necessarily have to renovate it to the standards you would use for an interior room in the house. Thinner-than-standard drywall will likely suffice and will be an economical choice (you'll want to insulate and clad the ceiling as well). You can upgrade windows or, if budget is a pressing concern, use a product such as insulating film to make the windows more weathertight.

Most local codes don't regulate modest, non-structural changes to an existing standalone shed—although you should always check with the local building department before starting the actual work to convert your shed into an office. The one big change you may need to make—one that will probably require hiring a professional and getting a permit—is running power to an unpowered shed. Using an extension cord as a power source for a shed is not an acceptable option because you'll quickly overload the cord capacity and circuit, and extension cords should not be left outdoors, unprotected, for long-term use.

A tidy, structurally sound existing garden shed can easily be converted into a simple, functional home office.

Depending on your available space and budget, you can choose a full-blown backyard structure that offers your home office an abundance of room and comes complete with hookups for electricity, lighting, and even plumbing.

## New building

This option gives you the chance to customize your home office to precisely suit what you do and how you prefer to work. It's also the opportunity to add quality-of-life features, such as large, sun-filled windows, skylights, and other extras that can make your workday more pleasant. However, all those advantages come at a steep price. Explore the possibilities by thinking about the following issues:

- What size structure do you really need, and will your existing property comfortably accommodate it?
- What restrictions do local ordinances and zoning codes put on this type of new outbuilding?
- Are you willing and able to sketch or create detailed drawings of the building, of high enough quality to be accepted by the local building department?
- Do you have a local contractor you trust who has a reputation for quality work?

- Are you capable and confident enough to do finishing work, such as hanging drywall and painting the structure (another money saver)?
- Is there a possibility of easily converting the building into a useful space (such as guest quarters) once it is no longer used as a home office or when you move?

Although you can hire a builder (or tackle the project yourself if you're an experienced DIYer and craftsman), the easier—if more expensive—option is a turnkey prefab shed package. Prefab room sheds (as opposed to storage sheds) range from the basic to the exceptionally luxurious, and many manufacturers offer some flexibility in the designs they offer. Most of these sheds come ready for electrical connection. The manufacturer ships the shed to your location, and most manufacturers maintain a network of local installers who will bid on the project and have experience installing prefab room sheds.

A standalone shed is a significant investment. It is best for a home-based entrepreneur or professional who needs a full-service office with room for expansion. This option is extremely attractive for anyone who prefers or needs to have complete isolation from the home proper but still be in close proximity.

When you introduce a substantial structure into your yard, you have to be careful not to create an eyesore in the landscape. This may seem likely a purely aesthetic consideration, but it will actually impact the market perception of your home. The easiest way to help the shed blend in—and avoid having a negative impact on property value—is by matching or at least complementing the home's exterior paint color. Landscaping around the shed will also help it appear as a natural addition to the property.

You don't necessarily need a huge shed if you're opting for a prefab all-in-one option like this backyard home office. A smaller shed often offers all the space most home offices need, taking up a more yard-friendly footprint.

## Permits and Pros

Whether you're converting an existing room into a full-fledged office or building a new shed to house your growing business, the first question to ask is: "Do I need a permit?" There's no reason to risk a fine or a stop-work order when a quick trip to the building department can answer that question. Generally, though, if you're making any structural changes, or altering a service—electrical or plumbing—you're likely to need a permit.

Not comfortable with doing the work yourself? You can leave the permitting to whatever professional you hire. The key word there is "professional." Whether you are planning on hiring a general contractor, or just need the services of a plumber or an electrician, be absolutely certain that the pro is both licensed and insured. You'll need proof of both.

# Heating and Cooling

Controlling the temperature and air quality in your workspace is important whether your office is in an existing room of your home, you are renovating a utility space such as a basement or attic, or your office is in a dedicated shed or other outbuilding. Solutions can range from a dehumidifier to a full mini-split HVAC (heating, ventilation, and air-conditioning) system.

## Heating

A space heater is a natural choice for heating any single room office or area. Keep in mind that warm air rises, so high ceilings in your office will mean that you may need a more powerful heater. The wattage rating on any heater is a good indication of capacity; a good general way to determine the wattage of the heater you need is to multiply the square feet of the space by 10.

You can choose from many different heating element designs. Convection heaters use a fan to circulate air over an internal heating element and then out into the space. These are best as whole-room heaters and for warming spaces like a shed home office. Radiant heaters don't have a fan and simply radiate heat outward from the elements; you may be able to find them in a wall-mountable form to save valuable desk or floor space. These include both electrical wire heaters and infrared units and are best for spot heating where it's particularly cold, like at your desk. You can also purchase oil-filled floor units that look like miniature radiators. Micathermic heaters feature a fanless technology that combines convection and radiant heating, circulating air through a natural convection process. For any heating unit, look for a cool-to-touch casing where you'll inevitably brush up against it and automatic shutoff switches to prevent overheating or in the event the unit falls over. Quiet technology, a programmable thermostat, and energy-conserving modes are all great features and worth paying extra for.

A simple radiant heater like this is great for "spot" heating, such as warming your legs or upper body.

An alternative to a heating unit is heated flooring. Usually heated flooring must be installed underneath the flooring you'll be walking on, which can be a good solution if you're renovating a space or creating a shed home office. Otherwise, consider a small electric foot warmer mat to keep your extremities warm with minimal fuss.

## Cooling

The most basic cooling technology for any home office involves windows and fans. An overhead fan can be surprisingly effective if you live in a relatively cool region. However, warmer months may require air conditioning in an attic, outbuilding, or south-facing room. An air conditioner placed in a window gives you excellent control of the room's temperature. If a window-mounted unit is not feasible, you can use a freestanding "portable" air conditioner that is vented through a hose connected to a window bracket. Both window and portable units can include extra features as the price goes up, such as a built-in dehumidifier, remote control, or activated carbon air filters.

A mini-split can provide heat, air-conditioning, and air circulation to a single room or space such as a shed home office.

## HVAC system

Utility spaces such as basements, attics, and garages can be dream home offices because you can completely customize them. But these spaces are often unheated and rarely include any kind of efficient ventilation. If you're willing to spend the money, you can extend the home's HVAC system to your office; doing so will likely require upgrading the entire house's system. However, if the heating and cooling options covered above aren't sufficient and you can't renovate the entire HVAC system, consider installing a mini-split unit. This is installed through the wall and supplies heat, AC, and a fan. The energy costs are limited to the one unit, and the unit is easy to control for maximum comfort, with direction fans, speed and blower power controls, and specific temperature settings.

# CHAPTER 2

# SETTING UP YOUR HOME OFFICE

Once you have chosen the perfect place to put

your home office, it's time to start designing it.

You'll need to make decisions about

the floor plan, your desired desk layout,

technology needs, and furniture. You'll also need to make

decisions about color and decoration to ensure your office is a place

where you'll want to spend significant amounts of time.

Built-in or custom storage units are a wonderful way of ensuring you have all the storage you could possibly need in a workspace, with a look that is unified and attractive.

# THE PLAN

Before you can form an area or room into your vision of the perfect home office, you need to know the particulars of that space. That means the dimensions, the placement of openings in the room, the location of services such as electrical outlets and phone jacks, and the light exposures. The first step is to accurately measure the available space. Note the square footage and the height of the ceiling. Measure the entire room, even if you're only planning on co-opting a corner or dividing it off into office space and a general-use area. Do this to give yourself an accurate overview of how the office will work for you and how it will impact and integrate into the overall room and the house at large.

Your floor plan need not be as detailed as this one, but the more details and precise measurements you can include, the more you'll head off any issues with furniture sizes, lighting, and power supply.

## Sketch it!

Now get out a sketchpad, a large piece of grid, graph, or sketch paper, or even a lined tablet. Grab a pencil—not a pen, because you want to be able to erase as necessary. Use the measurements you've just taken to create a rough outline for your basic room sketch. Most people find it easiest and most useful to scale the measurements 1 foot to 1 inch. You can really use whatever scale you want, but the sketch should be as large as possible for you to wind up with the most effective and useful overview.

When you have the outline and basics of the room nailed down, start adding details. Some people use furniture cutouts to make it easier to reconfigure the layout and try different furniture positions, but you can simply draw in where you would like to place your office desk, chair, and storage. Then start adding the existing furniture that will stay in the room. However, make sure the furniture is correctly proportioned. You don't have to be super detailed for this stage; basic block shapes to represent different furnishings will work fine.

Next, mark the position of the windows and doors, including a swing arc to note the direction a door opens. Make a note of the direction each window faces. Now measure and mark openings for any file drawers or other storage features in the room. Lastly, make small notes of the locations of wired-in light fixtures, electrical outlets, and phone jacks if applicable. Now, on a separate sheet, or to the side of your drawing, write up a key to the sketch. Below is an example of a finished sketch.

## Light exposure

It's vitally important to understand the natural light exposure in the room you choose for your home office. First, and most crucial, most people work during the day. That means that natural light is almost continuously affecting the workspace. A naturally bright office can create a feeling of well-being and is generally more attractive and conducive to work in than a dark, gloomy, cloistered space would be. This is the reason southeast or easterly exposures are preferable for a home office.

Beyond the general exposure, though, you'll need to consider how the sunlight comes in through the window. The sun is usually lower in the sky in winter. That's something to consider when planning your home office

and especially the position of any monitors or computer screens in the room. Ask the following questions before you commit to your layout:

- Does the sunlight coming in through a window heat up any one spot more than others in the room? (If your chair is there, you will eventually be uncomfortable.)
- What angle does the light come in through the window at different times during the day? This may take a bit of observation to answer, but it can head off a lot of frustration in the long run.
- Would the sun ever be directly in your eyes where you've placed your work chair?
- Does the sun shine in behind where you would be sitting, or at an oblique angle that would create screen glare? Keep in mind that even if the answer is "yes," it doesn't necessarily mean you have to find a new location for your office setup. You can moderate intense sunlight with blinds or curtains.

You'll supplement the natural light in your home office by an informed choice of artificial lighting fixtures. Learn more about assessing your artificial lighting needs, choosing what fixtures go where, and other lighting details on page 87.

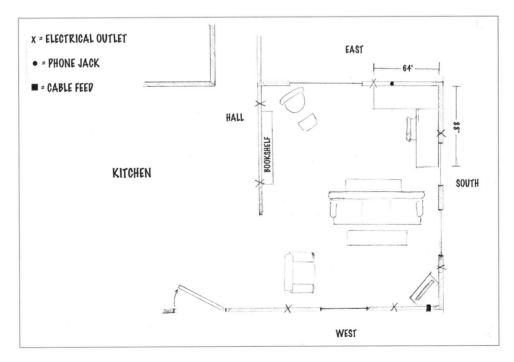

# 3D FLOOR PLAN IDEAS

Even with a 2D floor plan, some people still have difficulty determining what the actual space will be like—for instance, how the area between the front of a file cabinet and the edge of a sofa might be too confined to fully open the drawer and access files at the back. For that level of visualization, you may want to turn to 3D renderings.

Unless you're an artist, creating one by hand is going to be an insurmountable challenge. Don't fret. This type of detailed dimensional sketch can be created with many modern home design software packages. Today's programs routinely offer the capability to create 3D CAD (computer-aided design) floor plans such as the ones shown in this section. They are fantastic tools for visualizing exactly what the space will be like to live in with the home office placed in different areas. You can

preview the room on a monitor, and you can save yourself the hassle of having to upend a room in your house and move furniture around only to have to move it all again. If you want to make your own CAD floor plans, you can buy and learn a program, or you can use an online service.

The options on the following pages are examples of common room sizes and shapes. The details in your space may be different, but the principles that are involved in making decisions—and the ease with which you can troubleshoot and preview the room's layout—are typical of 3D floor plans. The important takeaway here is to "read" the floor plan—see the weaknesses and strengths you can build on to streamline the process of creating a home office.

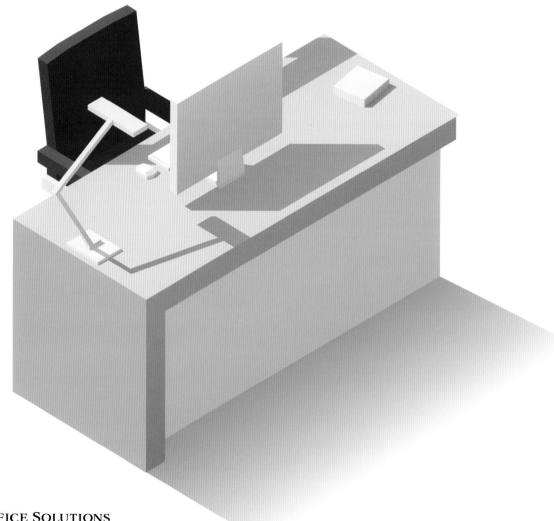

This type of 3D room view can be especially effective for laying out a small room such as this living room. Here, the desk has been placed to eliminate glare from the east-facing window, and pushing the front of the desk against the wall opens up the space and visual feel of the room. For the same reason, a trestle desk, which has open trestle-style legs as shown, was used; the open legs maintain the flow of light and air and add to the open and bright aesthetic.

An L-shaped room can be tricky to design and lay out, and even trickier to envision. Here, the desk is divorced from the relaxation area, making best use of what might otherwise be a dead area.

An L-shaped desk is an extravagance for any home office and should be carefully integrated into an existing space to cause the least amount of disruption with a maximum of efficiency. It can be challenging to center your home office around such a large work surface. Movement between the couch and desk in this room is going to be tight, and if the desk has to stay, the casual seating in the room should perhaps be changed.

The workspace here efficiently places the desk along an unbroken wall, and the home office dominates the room. If the worker were willing to streamline to a much a smaller desk and chair, those could be nested into the shelf alcove, freeing up abundant square footage.

This particular layout could be effective in a seldom-used guest bedroom or modest shared space such as a family room. The front of the desk and back of the monitor impose a separation that visually creates two distinct spaces in the room. Cable clutter, in an arrangement such as this, must be dealt with thoughtfully, and you need to pay attention to the window exposure to avoid monitor glare during the workday.

In home offices with a little extra space, adding a comfortable oversized chair and coffee table can get you out from behind the desk to an alternative spot to work when you're looking to break up the monotony. It's also a spot for young visitors to sit and color while you finish a report.

Even when an entire room is dedicated to a home office, it's essential that you carefully work out the ideal layout. The right placement of furnishings will ensure that work there is not only comfortable, but also viable in the long run. Here, the desk placement allows for a maximum of fluid, easy traffic flow. Its position in relation to the window takes advantage of the exposure throughout the day. In relation to the door, the desk is put in a formal orientation, to greet anyone coming into the room and leave no doubt that it's a workspace.

If you're going to commit an entire room to a home office, you should take advantage of any pleasing views from the room. Here, the desk placement does just that, while avoiding glare and hotspots from the natural light. This is also a fairly efficient layout; everything the worker needs is within a short roll of the chair. The easy chair is isolated and, although not far from the work surface, provides a quick and comfortable place to take regular breaks from the computer screen.

One of the most common arrangements in a home office, placing the desk in the corner allows you to use square footage that is often dead space to good advantage as a relatively isolated work area. Here, the arrangement of the rest of the furniture has not been perfected, but the desk is quite obviously right at home.

A corner L-shaped desk configuration is an excellent way to integrate a tech-heavy work setup into a bedroom—especially a long, narrow bedroom. The corner limits the visual disruption of the work area and allows for maximum work surface on which to place multiple monitors, accessories, scanners, and other essential, regularly used equipment.

Master bedrooms are not the first choice for a home office because the purpose of the room is the exact opposite of being industrious. However, if you don't have other options, this alternative can work if done with thoughtfulness and foresight. For psychological reasons, it's always wise to face the desk away from the bed so that you don't see the sleep area during work hours. In any case, place the desk as far as possible from the bed.

You can use a home office layout to put the focus on work and to screen distractions by simply facing the desk against a wall and using the wall space for storage. That leaves work necessities at your fingertips and ensures you don't end up staring at a TV from across the room. The file cabinet here was used to create a visual divider and further isolate the desk area. It's a wise move to locate the desk near a window, as well, because natural light promotes a mentally and physically healthy workspace.

# DESK LAYOUT

Once you've settled on the perfect location for your home office, it's time to deal with the desk layout. This will have a big impact on the rest of the furniture you choose for your home office. If you already own the furniture you want to incorporate, layout will mean balancing the positioning of the desk, chair, and storage with the size and shape of the allotted area.

The primary consideration in workspace layout is the desk configuration. The work surface (or surfaces) is usually the largest piece of furniture. It becomes the anchor of the layout and design. Putting a desk in the right place is crucial to ensuring that the work environment is comfortable and efficient. This is your chance to head off a lot of frustration in your workday.

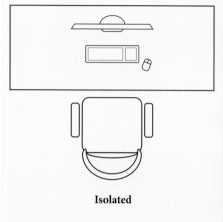

**Isolated**

## Isolated desk

This is one of the most common home office setups and perhaps the most flexible in terms of being able to adapt to any room. The desk can be built-in, along a wall such as in a kitchen, or in a room facing out with your back to a wall. Placing the desk is a matter of orienting it out of traffic flow and taking advantage of natural light in the space. The desk should also be placed so that you have handy access to any storage in the room where frequently used materials are kept (it's why a lot of home office isolated desks are placed in front of bookshelves). This option works best for anyone who does the vast majority of their work at their desk.

Two isolated desks make the best use of the available space in this room to allow for double workstations. There simply wasn't enough room for any other configuration to make sense and allow for reasonable movement of traffic into and out of the room and for the chairs to roll around behind the desks. This is an example of why isolated desks are the most common configuration for a home office.

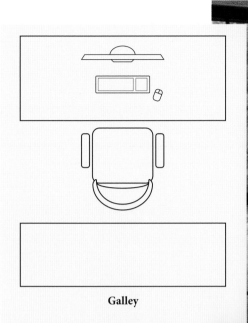

**Galley**

## Galley

The galley configuration is a great choice for anyone who needs a large work surface and especially those who only use a computer half the time or less. The layout includes two desks or work surfaces positioned parallel to one another. The worker sits between the two. The advantage is that by just turning the chair around, the worker can access the second work surface. This can be a benefit to someone who switches back and forth between tasks, such as an editor who reads galleys and then works on the computer, or a lawyer who reads briefs or legal documents and then writes up summaries on a laptop. Be aware that as attractive as it might be for your work process, a galley office takes up a lot of floor space.

A galley office such as this can be incredibly efficient. The worker need only turn around for extra desktop space to hold books or paperwork to be worked on later. The desk in front is the main work surface where the computer finds a home.

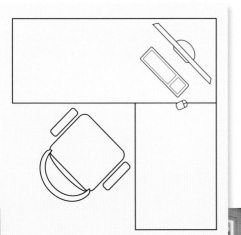

**L-shaped**

## L-shaped

This is an excellent choice for anyone who never has enough work surface, loves to spread out, regularly moves between monitors, documents, and reference materials, and needs to integrate an office into a larger existing room. The "L" can be formed by a large desk fabricated with a short side desk, or it can be created by butting two full-size desks up to each other. In either case, this configuration is naturally suited to nest into a corner. This means you can get a lot of work surface or storage in a location that is often dead space in any room.

This office is in the process of being set up. The L-shaped desk is important enough to the worker that it is the first thing to be placed; all else will follow around it.

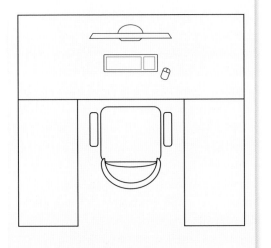

**U-shaped**

## U-shaped

Need a "command center" for all the work you do? A U-shaped configuration may be the option for you. This provides the maximum work surface in a hyper-efficient layout that puts everything you might use in your job within easy reach. The downside? Space. A U-shaped desk takes up an exceptional amount of square footage, especially if you're adding a couple of chairs for visitors or coworkers on the outside of the desk. Not only is the desk itself gigantic, but the area you need to move in and around the desk will be substantial. In most cases, U-shaped desks are only used in home offices that occupy an entire room, and this is the least common desk configuration. However, this can be an ideal solution for a busy graphic artist who needs to really spread out, or anyone whose work calls for more than one large computer monitor.

A U-shaped desk is ideal when you simply need a ton of workspace with many items right at your fingertips. The sacrifice is space—you'll need a lot of it to fit your desk(s) and be able to get in and out of the office. But if you have the space, this could be a very comfortable setup for you.

# TECHNOLOGY CHECKLIST

Love it or not, technology is a central player in most home offices these days. The type and amount of technology depends on what you do for a living, but here is the truth about the equipment you'll use in your work: as much as creating a home office is about designing an ideal workspace where comfort meets productivity, it is also a golden opportunity to consider your technical and equipment needs and put together the ideal setup that will make your work easier, more enjoyable, and more fruitful. You also might discover that there are new programs, applications, and digital ways of working that can streamline your work process and make what you do for a living easier and less time consuming (see Useful Applications and Programs, page 120).

This section divides your potential technology choices into Definitely Need, Might Need, and Beyond the Basics. Keep in mind that every worker will have different and personal needs that might mean these categories don't strictly apply to you, but it will get you off to a good start.

## Definitely Need

Let's face it: a **computer** is the one tool almost everyone working from home will need. Although "tower" desktop computers are still a standard in offices across the country, they are increasingly being replaced by just as powerful units that combine the monitor and keyboard in one freestanding piece of technology (known as "all-in-one" computers). And then you have current-generation laptops that rival any other computers for pure computing power in a much physically smaller package. Putting together a new home office is the perfect time to upgrade or switch to a new computer. Consider the following three options for choosing and designing around a type of computer.

**Desktops.** There is no getting around the fact that desktop computers with separate towers are space hogs. A tower should also be positioned to allow for reasonable airflow to cool the unit and extend the working life of the electronic components. If you currently own a slow, aging tower computer, creating a home office might be the perfect reason to update to an all-in-one or even a laptop.

**Laptop.** Not sure you're going to be working from home long-term? A laptop may be the ideal choice for your home office. The drawback to a laptop for most people is monitor size. Even larger models won't match the screen size you'll enjoy with upscale all-in-ones or high-end computer monitors. A larger monitor may be an essential if your work requires a spacious screen and realistic graphics. Keep in mind, though, that most laptops can be connected to a larger monitor.

**All-in-one.** This is a sleek alternative to the traditional tower-and-monitor desktop combination. The stand-mounted flat-screen monitor is built with the computing electronics inside the panel. Some models can even be wall-mounted. This makes them a wonderful option for small spaces where vertical surfaces may be available and desktop real estate is precious.

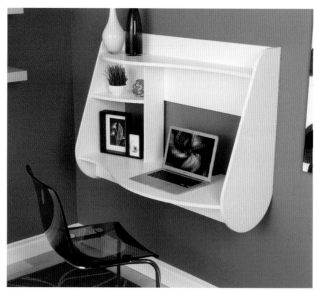

A laptop is an excellent option for space-challenged home offices and limited surface areas, such as the desk on this wall-mounted unit. These days, laptops can do most everything a desktop unit can and serve the purpose for many people working from home.

In modest spaces, and especially where extra storage is limited, like in this off-the-kitchen office, an all-in-one computer can be both a stylish and practical work solution.

## Might Need

Many people find the inclusion of these technology items to really improve the quality of their work day. They may not be essential, but they could be truly beneficial.

### Printer/scanner/copier

As with all things computer-related, basic office printers continue to get smaller and smaller. That's good news for space-challenged home office designers. The other continuing trend is toward all-in-one units that include scanning and copying capabilities. The standard for home office tasks is an inkjet printer, but if you're a graphic professional or someone like a real estate agent, you may need a laser printer for higher-quality printouts for your work. These are normally bulkier and require room for printout ejection and fan vents.

Today's personal printers not only come with an amazingly small footprint, but many also offer scanning and copying capabilities—all for a price that can fit inside just about any home office budget.

### Keyboards and mice

Upgrading to a wireless keyboard and mouse is a wonderful way to keep cords out of your way while working, not to mention making the home office look neater and more streamlined. If you work on the computer all day long, it is worth looking into an ergonomic keyboard designed to take stress off your hands.

### Speakers and headphones

Your computer's internal speakers might suffice for your current needs. But if you listen to music throughout the day, or plan on participating in regular video meetings, an upgrade to external speakers or to a quality set of headphones may be warranted. Most external speakers are relatively small and will easily fit on top of most desks. Headphones with a built-in microphone can be especially useful for those professionals who participate in frequent video meetings and conferences.

External speakers may be a necessity in order to guarantee that you'll hear everything said in a videoconference meeting clearly enough to make notes and react.

# Beyond the Basics

Whether or not you're interested in the following tech items will largely depend on your particular job. But it is worth noting that all of these can be extremely useful for anyone who regularly works on a computer and wants their digital duties to be as quick and trouble-free as possible.

## External hard drive

Any external hard drive offers two benefits: additional storage and compartmentalized backup. These devices usually require efficient air circulation around them to keep them from overheating. However, if you use a cloud-based (online) backup service, you may not need this piece of equipment.

## Hubs

A cable hub is more of an organizational tool than an actual tech necessity. It is a center point for your computer setup, where multiple peripherals can be plugged in, so that a single cable can be routed to the computer. These add-ons can go a long way toward eliminating cord clutter and making the home office more attractive.

## Battery backup

A short interruption in electrical power, like a power outage caused by a car running into a power pole, can mean that you lose a lot of valuable work. Battery backups insure against those possibilities. They are not very attractive, so, whenever possible, it's best to conceal one in a cabinet. Make sure it has good air circulation around it to keep it from overheating.

## External camera

Most jobs involve some interaction with colleagues, clients, or other professionals. Today, that increasingly means meeting through videoconferences. Even though many modern computers come with a camera built into the unit, yours may not have one, or the quality may be unacceptable. In that case, you'll need to buy an external camera. They are usually mounted on top of a monitor and wired directly to the computer.

External hard drives are small but essential peripherals, part of many automatic backup programs. Most derive power through the cord that connects them to the computer, which limits cord clutter.

A hub is an excellent way to make for quick laptop disconnects and to keep all your various tech cables organized.

# Wireless Working

Most home offices today use a wireless network in which the Internet router sends out a radio signal to devices on the network (in what's called a wireless local area network, or WLAN). There is a reason wireless technology has become the widespread standard not only in corporate offices but in home offices as well. If you have older equipment that must be physically connected to one another and the router, you'll be limited in where you can place that equipment. Nobody wants to have computer cables sprawling across the floor to a shelf on the opposite wall.

However, there are strong arguments to be made against using your home wireless network to serve your home office. First, home Internet service is often slower than business high-speed connections. If you're working with larger electronic files, or uploading and downloading files on a regular basis, you may be noticeably more efficient with a high-speed connection. At moments when the rest of the family is using the Internet connection to stream movies, play online games, or browse the web, your service may slow down. Isolating your online work will also make calculating and taking tax deductions much easier.

Lastly, you can better guarantee the security of an online connection when it is dedicated to your business. For these reasons, you can consider setting up a separate wireless network for your home office.

Regardless of how your wireless is set up, you may need an extender—also called boosters, repeaters, or wireless access points—to keep the signal strong at your computer. Extenders amplify the signal from the router. They are a way to keep your connection strong even when the router is relatively far away or blocked by walls and other surfaces.

Wireless extenders come in many sizes and shapes, and usually in cream, white, or black. Some, like this one, plug directly into a wall outlet, keeping the unit well out of the way and off surfaces where it might get knocked around.

## The Scan Life

Want to make your work easier and your home office less cluttered? Want to get more organized with a simple change to your work process that will save you time and effort (and maybe even money)? Look no further than a document scanner (or, perhaps, your phone).

Rather than filing paper documents, most of what you need to keep and reference can be scanned. You can do this simply by creating a digital file folder structure on your computer and using your scanner or all-in-one unit to scan a copy of any paperwork into the right computer folder. That's the most basic option.

But if you're willing to spend a tiny sum on a scanning organization program, your scans can be even more useful. You'll find programs that replicate documents from images you shoot with your phone camera—a quicker and easier option than actually scanning a piece of paper. You can also buy programs that will convert your scanned documents into searchable and editable text. That can come in mighty handy when you can't remember where you stored an older document on your computer. For several options, see Useful Applications and Programs on page 120.

# Containing Cord Chaos

Wireless technology offers a way to free the home office from much of the cable and cord clutter that can be such a nuisance in small workspaces. However, you may not yet have embraced the wireless life. Even if you have, power cords will remain an issue for some time to come. Fortunately, there are many solutions on the market to help you deal with that issue. The options below can also be used throughout the house to manage cord clutter in places like your home entertainment center.

## Ties

The simplest way to corral cords and cables is to bind them together. The simplest way to do that is by zip-tying them. Zip ties are inexpensive and sold in different lengths, so you can find ties that are ideal even if you have to manage several thick cables. When it comes time to remove or replace equipment, or disconnect for any reason, a zip tie is easily cut with side-cutting pliers or plain old wire cutters.

## Cord sleeves/tubes

Another way to bundle multiple cords or cables together is to use inexpensive sleeves. Some are just fabric tubes through which you slide the cables; others are plastic spirals that are wound around multiple cables. Either type keeps cables from sprawling. Cord conduit is a metal tube through which cables are run. Conduit has to be fixed to a wall or other surface. Some manufacturers build cord organizers into furniture, including filing cabinets and desks.

## Hangers, clips, and channels

These offer even neater options to keep multiple cords and cables in order. They are local solutions, meaning they can be used all along the length of different cords, or just at the desk or other point where the cords all converge and jumble up. Hangers are screwed or stuck to a solid surface such as the underside of a desk, and a single cord is hung from each hook. Clips and channels come in self-adhesive and non-stick versions; individual cords or cables are just snapped into place.

Simple, inexpensive organizers like this provide home office value far beyond their modest price tags. Self-adhesive versions can be attached to just about any metal, plastic, or wood vertical surface—or even the underside of a desk—to keep multiple cords in order and ready for connection.

The most basic, inexpensive option for running cords or cables along walls or moldings—or even structures such as wainscoting—cable clips are just what they sound like: individual screw-mounted clips that leave the cable or cord exposed, but hold it in place and route it. They aren't an elegant solution, but if you're looking for pure functionality with a minimal cost and super easy installation, clips could serve your needs.

No matter how you organize them, it's always a good idea to label cords or cables (other than the power cable) so that you know exactly which is which when it comes time to disconnect a peripheral or piece of equipment. You can label cables with handwritten file folder peel-and-stick labels, or you can use special cord identifiers widely available through office supply chains and online.

# HOME OFFICE FURNITURE

Setting up most home offices will require buying some new furniture. However, you may already have the bones of your home office furniture suite waiting to be pressed into service. Most people own a work desk and chair. It is worth asking, however, "Are they the right work desk and chair?" And there are many other furniture pieces to consider. Investing in the appropriate home office furnishings isn't just a matter of aesthetics or convenience; those choices will have a big impact on how comfortable and productive you are while you work.

Much as home office furniture must primarily accommodate how you work and keep you comfortable, it also has to blend in seamlessly with the other furnishings in your house. At the very least, home office essentials should not stick out like a sore thumb in the interior design.

There are really three directions to pick from when you're choosing exactly what desk, chair, and storage you'll include in your home office: blend, match, or highlight. Most people either select those that will simply disappear into the room, being so bland or understated that they don't call attention to themselves (blend), or opt for pieces that effectively fit with other furniture, fixtures, and finishes, complementing what's already in the home (match). But if you have a fearless design ethic and a sense of decorative adventure, you can always choose work furnishings that stand out for their own design panache (highlight). The best place to start in pursuit of any of these goals is with the centerpiece of the home office—the desk.

Corner desks are a great way to have side-by-side workstations, or just a lot of room to spread out, in an economical footprint. A desk like this can work in spaces small and large and can be a wonderful way to exploit the dead area some room corners represent.

# Desks

The desk is usually the command center for the professional work we do, and it is certainly the center point of any home office. Choosing the perfect desk ensures that you have everything you might need at any time during the workday right at hand. A work desk should be sized correctly for the available space and provide all the top surface you'll need. It should offer clearance underneath not only for your legs, but for any rolling storage you might want to use. It can be wise to plan on dropping a little bit more money to buy a desk outfitted with the latest extras—features such as concealed desktop outlets, built-in cable organizers, or even adjustable legs. The additional cost will pay off in convenience. Ultimately, though, your decision will largely be driven by size and shape. A desk with the proper dimensions will foster an ergonomic sitting position, reduce eye strain, and spur productivity. That's a lot to ask from one basic piece of furniture.

A visit to any furniture store or even an office supply outlet will quickly reveal that you have abundant desk options from which to choose. There are not only a full range of materials and styles, but overall size and shape vary widely as well. Where desks in corporate buildings all over the country tend to resemble one other, the selection available to the home office outfitter is anything but limited. Still, there is a reason why most business furniture desks are manufactured to a traditional set of dimensions. It's just a matter of the science behind how people sit and work at a desk. Researchers and manufacturers have worked long and hard to discover exactly how much space someone's legs need under a desk and how much elbow room they'll require to write comfortably on a pad of paper, type on a keyboard, or move a mouse. Here are the tried-and-true standard dimensions for a work desk:

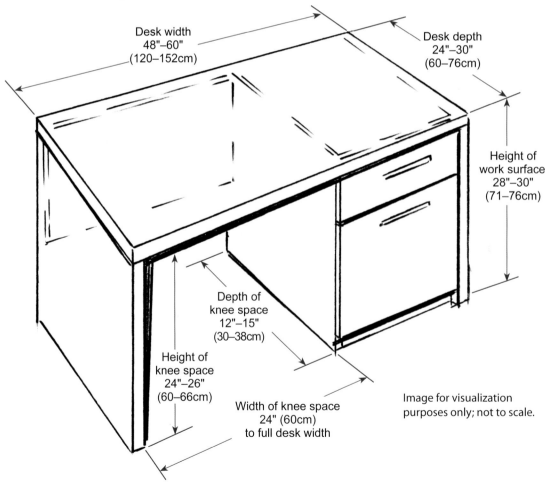

Desk width
48"–60"
(120–152cm)

Desk depth
24"–30"
(60–76cm)

Height of
work surface
28"–30"
(71–76cm)

Depth of
knee space
12"–15"
(30–38cm)

Height of
knee space
24"–26"
(60–66cm)

Width of knee space
24" (60cm)
to full desk width

Image for visualization
purposes only; not to scale.

These measurements are excellent starting points. The standard, of course, isn't one size fits all, though. Choose a size and structure that suit your individual needs. Use other furniture in the house to get ideas of what measurements will and won't work for you if you are going to be ordering something online and won't have a chance to see it in person.

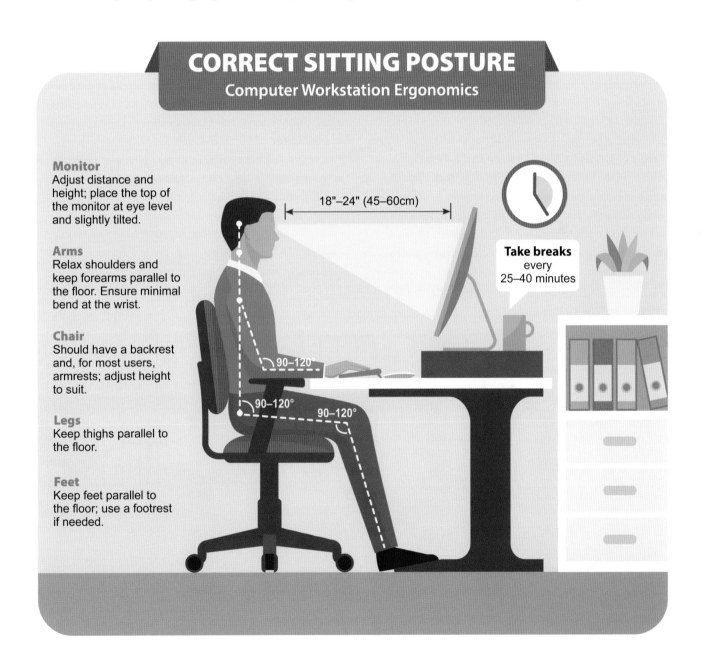

# CORRECT SITTING POSTURE
## Computer Workstation Ergonomics

**Monitor**
Adjust distance and height; place the top of the monitor at eye level and slightly tilted.

**Arms**
Relax shoulders and keep forearms parallel to the floor. Ensure minimal bend at the wrist.

**Chair**
Should have a backrest and, for most users, armrests; adjust height to suit.

**Legs**
Keep thighs parallel to the floor.

**Feet**
Keep feet parallel to the floor; use a footrest if needed.

18"–24" (45–60cm)

**Take breaks** every 25–40 minutes

90–120°
90–120°
90–120°

## Materials

If you don't already have a desk that meets your needs, you'll find an amazingly wide and diverse selection at retail. Desks are also some of the most common pieces for sale in classified ads or on sites such as Craigslist. A used desk can be an incredible cost-saving option. Often, they have seen little wear and are offered at a fraction of the original cost. Regardless of where you buy your desk, though, you'll first have to decide what material works best for you.

Metal is heavy and substantial, but most metal desks hardly qualify as "stylish." They are also cold to the touch, which can be unpleasant in the winter. Wood is the more common choice for good reason. A solid wood desk will last a long time, and, given the number of wood species and potential finishes, you can choose from an amazing range of surface appearances. The downside is that wood dents and scars. This can be an issue over time, as occasional equipment scratches and the banging of a rolling chair into a desk leg take their toll.

Glass desks are a sleek look for a modern or contemporary home office. There is a fair bit of sacrifice for the look, however. Glass desktops are famously difficult to keep clean, and a few drops of spilled coffee or the errant fingerprint mars the appearance. This option also rarely includes drawers or shelves, making glass desks less useful than other types. The surface can also be cold to the touch, which can be an issue in the winter—especially in colder areas of the country or colder locations in the house, such as a basement.

Composite desks are largely wood filler and plastic or, at the extreme low end of the market, melamine-wrapped particleboard. They're cheap and come in many different design styles, but the wear-and-tear of daily home office use shows on these desks long before it would on sturdier versions. Choose a prefab composite desk and you'll be trading significant initial cost savings for longevity.

A sleek, well-built desk like this sit-to-stand model with power adjustable legs (currently in the down position) leaves lots of space underneath for the handsome and ergonomically supportive chair to roll wherever it needs to go. The wood veneer surface is durable and fabricated to last.

## Storage needs

Desks aren't just work surfaces. A desk with drawers may supply all the extra storage you need in your home office. Generate a lot of paperwork in your job? Look for a desk with at least one file drawer. Use a range of art supplies in your work? Pick out a desk with a couple of shallow drawers right under the top, which you can customize with inserts. Locking drawers even provide some measure of security.

Drawers aren't the only form of storage a desk can offer. Some come with built-in shelves. These offer quick-access storage for paper supplies, notebooks, and files or books that you reference often in your work. Shelves on the opposite, non-work side of the desk can be used for storage or display and are considered a chic desk feature. Of course, if you've gone paperless (kudos!), the clean, streamlined look of a wood or glass desk with no drawers or shelves at all may be the ideal work surface and design statement.

Some of the handiest storage features aren't necessarily the most obvious. Slide-out keyboard trays that can be concealed under the desktop when not in use not only free up desktop space for other activities such as writing or reading, but also lower the level of the keyboard to what may be an ergonomically superior height for most users (your arms should ideally be bent at right angles when working on a computer keyboard).

This desk offers useful storage at one side but an open, airy space underneath, allowing for airflow and an attractive aesthetic.

## Specialized desks

The standard four-leg, one-top "writing" desk is far from the only style. In fact, another style of desk might suit your available space or the way you want to work better. For instance, **"ladder" desks** are designed to take up minimal floor space. Both the desk and storage shelves or cubbies are placed vertically. This type of desk can be an ideal solution for a small apartment where space is at a premium, or where you simply don't want to create a significant home office footprint in a larger space such as a living room or guest bedroom. Let's take a look at a variety of nonstandard desks you may want to consider.

**Floating desks** save a good deal of space. These are attached directly to a wall and usually have no legs, and no apparent support brackets. The look is clean, and floating desks are common in places like kitchens where the use and design of the room dominate the space and the home office is meant to blend in as completely as possible. A floating desk is also a good addition in a dual-use room like a guest bedroom. Word to the wise, though: if you're installing a floating desk, making sure it is properly secured into wall studs. The pressure over time of a person working, typing, writing, and leaning on the desktop will tend to pull it away from the mounting surface.

A compact wall-mounted desk is a space-saving solution ideal for apartment dwellers that only need a small amount of workspace.

This custom-made corner desk and home office was created with the help of a closet storage company that provided the sophisticated file cabinets and shelves to create a look that does this den-turned-workspace justice. A neutral color scheme and abudant work surface make this a pleasurable place to put in the hours earning a living.

**Armoire desks** offer a similar space-saving benefit. These self-contained units feature a drop-down or completely concealed desk with a roll-up or flip-up lid and abundant cubbies and shelves for small storage. Working on an armoire desk is an exercise in economy of motion. There isn't a lot of room for piles of paperwork or a large computer monitor. But if you're comfortable working with the limited space and perhaps on a laptop, you may find that an armoire keeps all your work materials within easy reach and secured when you're not working. With the lid closed, the right armoire home office will blend in with the rest of your furnishings quite convincingly.

**Corner desks** are some of the most useful and unusual home office options on the market. These allow you to take advantage of space that is often a dead zone in any large room. The configuration also provides a wealth of surface area for workers who have a lot of equipment they need to access often, or who just really prefer to spread out. Another advantage is that the copious surface area inevitably leaves a lot of space for a colleague or coworker to join you, or as somewhere to put rolling storage units.

**Rolling** or **"mobility" desks** are an uncommon option for home office workers. These types of desks have wheels and can be rolled to different areas in the house. Most workers opt for a laptop if they want pure portability, but a rolling desk allows you to take along paperwork or, if you have a high rolling desk, have a standing work surface wherever you go. A mobile desk works best if you don't use a computer, electronics, or peripherals in your work, because plugging and unplugging when you move the desk can become an irritation. If you choose this option, select a desk on which at least two of the wheels lock, so that you don't experience any unintended movement while working.

## Standing versus sit-to-stand desks

Sit-to-stand desks—those with adjustable or fixed legs that are taller than standard desk legs—have become increasingly popular over the last decade or so. Manufacturers and some experts tout the health benefits of working while standing at least part of the time. Although there isn't a large body of research on the topic, the practice may help with back problems and some other concerns (and it's a fact that you burn more calories when standing than when seated). However, standing in poor posture or on a hard surface for long stretches can cause more problems than it prevents. If you decide to stand at work, follow these five guidelines:

**1. Alternate.** Standing for hours at a time in any situation can be detrimental to your musculoskeletal system. When you first start using a standing desk, ease into the practice by standing for 15 to 20 minutes at a time, then sit for the same amount of time. If your legs get tired, you experience pain, or you begin slouching, sit to give your body a break. Increase the time as your body gets used to standing.

**2. Set the monitor.** Correct monitor viewing height is key to avoiding back problems whether you are sitting or standing. The monitor should be positioned so that the top of the screen is at eye level, with the screen tilted up toward your face about 20 degrees. The monitor should be 24 to 28 inches (60 to 71cm) from your face.

**3. Set the keyboard.** Your elbows should be bent 45 degrees with your fingers resting on the keyboard, and your arms should be slightly more extended then they would be if you were sitting. You may need to use a keyboard tray to ensure or maintain this relationship.

**4. Avoid hard, uneven surfaces.** You should be standing on a resilient surface that is firm but has some cushion. Better still, use an anti-fatigue mat that is designed specifically to alleviate stress on joints and muscles while standing.

**5. Take time-outs.** Whenever you're working on a computer, whether you're standing or sitting, take regular breaks about every 20 minutes. Take a couple minutes to stretch, walk around, and clear your head. You can even use the time to make business calls on your cell phone.

Because sitting for long periods is often not possible or even desirable, it's best to purchase a sit-to-stand desk that is fully adjustable (as most are). You can purchase a desk that itself raises and lowers in its entirety, or you can purchase a desktop model that sits on top of an existing desk, like this one.

The vast majority of modern standing desks offer the option of sitting part of the time, because the legs are adjustable down to a traditional writing desk height. Many of these models include controls that automatically raise or lower the legs at the push of a button. Because most workers alternate between sitting and standing, power controls can save a lot of time, effort, and frustration.

An alternative to a sit-to-stand desk—and a way to adjust monitor height for users of varying heights—is a traditional desk outfitted with a riser. This is a platform that rests on the top of the desk. The computer monitor is put on the riser, and most risers can be raised or lowered by way of scissor or extending legs in the base. Some risers include a pullout tray for a keyboard and mouse as an easy way to alternate between sitting and standing in seconds.

Most riser platforms are made for traditional computer monitors or all-in-one computers built into the monitor, but you can find risers like this one that accommodate laptops. These are useful for anyone who prefers the ease and portability of working full-time on a laptop, but who also wants to make sure the monitor level is appropriate when sitting to reduce eye and neck strain.

## Murphy and wall-mounted desks

Wall-mounted desks are in a category by themselves. They are meant to offer a workspace that takes up very little area, but they also must be installed correctly to ensure integrity and safety over the long run. They can be inexpensive options to creating an entire home office, and the space-saving benefits will be attractive to anyone who lives in a smaller home, such as a modest townhouse or condo.

Murphy desks are a less common type of wall-mounted home office solution. Like their namesake the Murphy bed, Murphy desks feature a fold-down lid that conceals the storage for the unit when closed, and provides a desk surface when open. There are some space and work constraints to a Murphy desk. To start with, if you're going to flip up the lid regularly at the end of the workday, you can't have a bunch of tech accessories or a tumble of paperwork on top of the desk. Like all wall-mounted desks, a Murphy desk is best partnered with a laptop computer. Peripherals like a printer are normally used wirelessly and kept elsewhere, such as on nearby bookshelves. Storage within the unit is typically limited both in the physical depth of the shelves or cubbies and in the actual total amount of storage.

The Murphy desk does, however, give you the chance to completely conceal your home office during your off-hours. Depending on the exterior look of the Murphy desk you choose—or how you customize it—it can visually disappear when not in use. You can even paint it the exact same color as the wall to create this effect. Of course, you can also use the underside of the lid as a canvas for a cool painted or stenciled design.

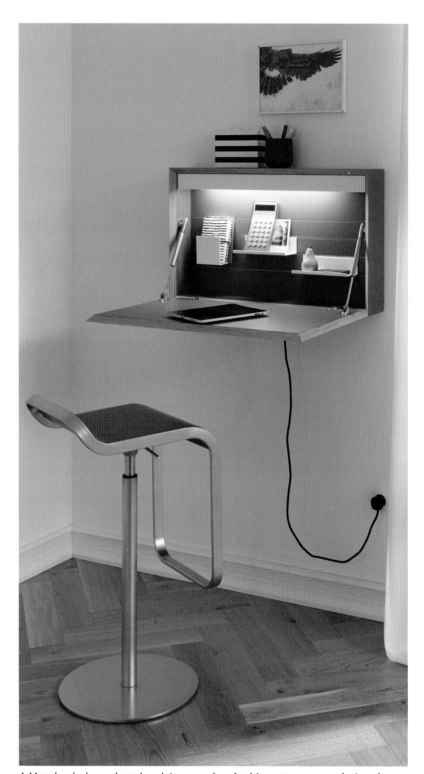

A Murphy desk need not be plain or stodgy. As this contemporary design shows, these types of compact home office options can be stylish and still contain a lot of useful storage in a small amount of space, along with a pull-down work surface.

Basic wall-mounted units without a flip-up lid are more common than Murphy units. These usually offer a modest amount of exposed storage and sometimes a cabinet or two. A shallow desk is built into the unit so that you face the wall when working. Basic wall-mounted units lend themselves to being supplemented with wall-mounted shelves or cabinets, more so than Murphy desks do. They are also a better home for a desktop computer, but for an acceptable appearance, you'll need to have a neat and organized work process. Any mess or clutter can easily become an eyesore with a wall-mounted home office unit.

Both Murphy desks and wall-mounted units exploit unused vertical space, but they require fastening into more than one stud. That may limit where you can mount the unit. In most cases, you'll also want to place them near a wall outlet, so that you can plug in computers, phone chargers, and peripherals as needed.

All-in-one wall-mounted desk options such as this can be an ideal space saver where your home doesn't have much extra space to accommodate a full-time work area. This unit is designed with enough desk surface to accommodate a large-screen computer as well as a separate tray for the keyboard and mouse.

# Chairs

Your office chair is not the place to save money. The right chair will reduce backache and eye strain, maintain productivity and energy levels, and ensure proper circulation. The wrong chair will do the opposite of all that. That's why it's not a great idea to repurpose a regular household chair as your full-time home office seating. An office chair is meant to explicitly support your body while you work—other chairs don't. The best office chairs are adjustable in several different areas for different parts of your body. Rolling chairs are the ideal, but they may not be right for every situation or may not fit into the design of every room.

## Wheels

The first choice you'll make in choosing an office chair will between one with legs or one with a wheeled base. In general, a wheeled chair will be more appropriate as a companion to a desk. A wheeled chair may also incur less wear and tear on the flooring under your desk. Wheels offer more flexibility and less effort in movement as well. The best chair wheels are independent roller-bearing casters, and the more caster legs—and consequently wheels—the chair has, the better. Although lower-cost chairs often have four wheels, five- or six-wheeled bases are optimal.

## Arms

Arms on an office chair are considered an ergonomic benefit. To get the most health value, though, it's best if the arms are adjustable so that they don't force your shoulders into an awkward or unhealthy position while you're sitting. All that said, you may prefer to work without arms on your chair if they make you feel constrained or uncomfortably enclosed.

The ribbed chair (at left) offers enough padding to make sitting comfortable, with gaps that allow hot or cold air to circulate around your body, keeping you comfortable throughout the day. The mesh chair (at right) allows a maximum of air circulation along with plenty of support for your back and legs. Both chairs include a full complement of adjustable features, including lumbar support, height and tilt adjustments, and arm height settings (on the chair at right).

## Material

The material of which your chair is made will have a big impact on comfort, chair longevity, and how ergonomic the chair is. Wood and plastic are usually the least expensive options (except in the case of antique wood office chairs), but they are also the worst options for your musculoskeletal system, not to mention your long-term comfort. Mesh is a popular option because it is so breathable and allows effective air circulation around the body. The mesh on lower-quality chairs— often knockoffs of designer office chairs—will begin to sag over time and become an ergonomic negative rather than a plus. Many home office workers prefer the comfort of a well-padded chair, which translates to a surface clad in leather or fabric upholstery. Fabric tends to wear quicker, look dirtier over time and use, and be more comfortable in colder temperatures than hotter climates. Leather breathes, is cleanable, and wears well, but it may be a little cold when the temperature of the office is on the low side (and it can be sticky when the temperature gets a bit too hot). Just keep in mind that padded surfaces will likely compact over time, becoming denser, harder, and less comfortable.

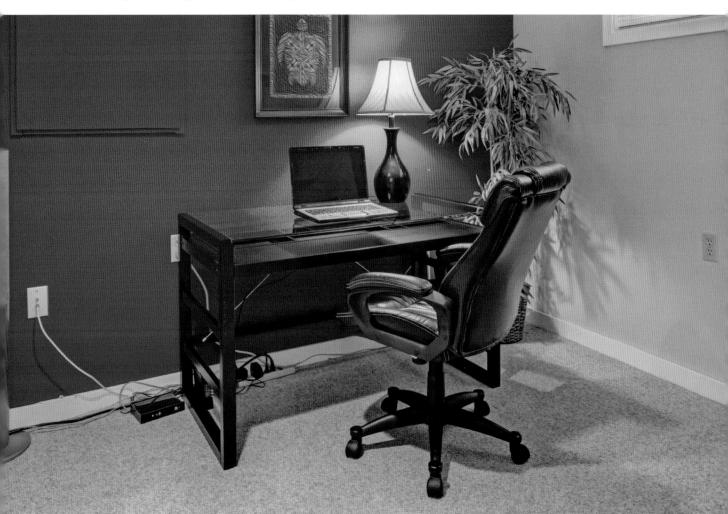

In this minimal basement office, the chair's arms and ample cushioning ensure that the chair is completely ergonomic and as comfortable to sit in during the last hour of the workday as it was during the first.

# Four Features of Quality Office Chairs

### Spine support

The back of the chair should follow the shape of your spine—a key factor in maintaining proper posture while you work. That one feature is also important to head off long-term issues with your neck and shoulders. Adjustable lumbar (lower back) support is a big plus in any chair. Being able to fine-tune your lower-back support will radically affect how comfortable you are in the chair over time, and your posture. A taller back is preferable, ideally with neck and head support. But at the very least, the back of the chair should come up to the midpoint of your shoulder blades.

### Adjustable seat

This is an absolute must-have for any home office worker. The correct seat height should allow your feet to rest flat on the floor (or on an ergonomic under-desk foot rest). A seat with memory foam padding is also a big plus, but be careful of low-quality memory foam that will quickly wear out and leave an impression of your legs and backside. A plain foam seat will also tend to compress over time and can create circulation issues in your upper legs and lower back. Make sure the seat is sized correctly for your body; there should be a gap of about 2 inches (5cm) between the inside of your knees and the front of the seat when you're sitting in the chair. A seat that is level or tilts very slightly forward is preferable, because that will foster the healthiest sitting position. Avoid seats that tilt noticeably backward.

### Proper armrests

Fixed armrests—those that don't move in, out, up, or down—are the sign of a cheap office chair. The more adjustable the armrests are, the better. The armrests should be fairly close to your body to avoid pinching your shoulders when your forearms are resting on the chair arms. Ideally, keep the armrests level with the height of the desk. That may seem a little high at first, but it's the best position for effective shoulder support.

### Sturdy base

As a general rule, the more wheels on an office chair, the better. The base should be solid construction rather than thin or hollow support arms for the casters. The chair should easily roll in any direction. Ball bearing casters are preferred for maximum wheel life; simple axles through a hole in the wheel have a much greater chance of breaking over time and use. Keep in mind that one broken wheel is usually all it takes to make the chair inoperable and of little value.

You'll notice your chair is set up correctly if, after working on a computer for more than thirty minutes, your neck and shoulders are still relaxed and your head isn't jutting forward toward the computer screen.

# Lighting

Getting the most of out of your home office means thinking carefully about how it will be lit and a how different fixtures in the room will affect your work. Start on your lighting game plan by considering the natural light in the space (because that's the type of lighting you have the least influence over). Note the intensity of the natural light throughout the day, particularly on the spot where you'll sit at your desk. Ask the following questions:

- Is any one time of day of particular concern?
- Will you need to add blinds or curtains to mute direct light?
- Do you participate in regular video meetings, and is the existing natural light conducive to that?

Next, consider where the task lighting should go. If you have a galley desk setup, a corner desk, or a particularly expansive work surface, you may need more than one task light fixture for different areas. Once you're confident that you have all the illumination you'll need at desk level, consider the ambient light fixtures in the room. Often, this is supplied by one ceiling-mounted fixture. Does the light from that fixture eliminate corner shadows and fill in behind the computer, making the screen easier on the eyes? You can always add ambient light with wall sconces, floor lamps, or even additional overhead fixtures. Finally, add accent lighting under cabinets, in bookshelves, or as you prefer to dress up the home office.

This modern shed office benefits from abundant windows but includes a well-thought-out lighting scheme for when the sun isn't shining brightly. An overhead track lighting fixture can be adjusted to direct halogen light to fill in shadows, while a sleek desk lamp ensures task lighting.

## Task lighting

Just as it sounds, this is bright, direct lighting specific to a work surface. In the home office, task lighting usually translates to a desk lamp, which is an absolute necessity. The best desk lamps are adjustable, so that you can direct the beam of light to different areas for different tasks. For instance, it's wise to light behind a computer screen while you work on it, and to shine light directly on any paperwork you're reading or writing. The name notwithstanding, a floor lamp—and even a wall-mounted fixture—can actually serve as a desk lamp if it is entirely adjustable and can focus a beam of light at any place on the desk. A dimmer is a handy feature for a desk lamp, as is a weighted base that will ensure the lamp doesn't tip over. Always place desk lamps opposite your dominant hand to prevent annoying shadows when you write or make notes.

An artistic gooseneck lamp is just right for this stunning, modern-themed, compact home office. The light features a powerful, energy-saving LED fixture and three brightness settings, ensuring that the worker will always have exactly the light he or she wants—and needs to avoid eye strain. The heavy base ensures the light is almost impossible to tip over and includes a USB port and electrical outlet, making it even handier than it already was.

## Ambient lighting

This is supplied by overhead fixtures, wall sconces, or floor lamps. Even though task lighting takes center stage in the home office, ambient lighting is important. The general light from ambient fixtures fills in shadows that might otherwise confuse the eye and increase eye strain. The key with ambient lighting is to make sure that the light source—the bulb—is the right type and wattage for the space and that it provides enough light to fill in where task lighting leaves off.

## Accent lighting

Strictly speaking, accent lighting isn't a necessity in a home office. This is lighting basically used for decorative effect, although it can provide a small bit of practical benefit as well. Shelf lights, under-cabinet lights, or even a motion lava lamp you sit on the desktop can all serve as accent lighting.

In this office, the task lighting is complemented by ambient lighting provided by a floor lamp as well as overhead ceiling lights, providing maximal flexibility.

## Light bulb types

Your home office lighting plan doesn't end after you've picked out the lighting fixtures. Just as important a decision is the type of light bulbs you'll use in those fixtures.

**LEDs**. Light-emitting diode bulbs are an energy-efficient alternative to standard incandescent bulbs (a 12-watt LED bulb is equivalent to the standard 60-watt incandescent bulb). They cost more but last significantly longer. LEDs generally produce a cooler, bluer light than the warm yellow glow of an incandescent bulb. You can, however, buy LEDs that produce the familiar warm light of an incandescent.

**CFL**. LED bulbs' closest competitors are compact fluorescent lamp, or CFL, bulbs. A CFL bulb will last longer than an incandescent but will have a significantly shorter lifespan than an LED bulb—as well as a significantly lower price. Today's CFL bulbs are color-corrected to mimic the familiar warm yellow glow of an incandescent bulb.

**Traditional fluorescent.** These bulbs, the precursor to modern CFLs, are the least desirable home office lighting. Even though there are now warm-color versions and even colored types, the light produced by standard fluorescents is usually cold and harsh. These bulbs cannot be dimmed, either.

**Incandescent.** The standard light bulbs for decades, incandescents remain wildly popular. Incandescent light is warm and welcoming, and higher-watt versions provide enough illumination for even fine detail work. Incandescent bulbs produce great fill lighting, banishing shadows and creating a glow that is easy on the eyes.

**Halogen.** Halogen bulbs are a type of incandescent light, but the light produced is not the same; it is a clean, bright, white light that makes details and colors pop in their truest form. This is an energy-efficient option and great for task lighting. Unfortunately, the bulbs produce significant amounts of heat, so it's not a good idea to use them in fixtures you might touch or bump into.

LED light bulbs come in many forms for different fixtures, including a standard bulb (far left) that can replace most incandenscent bulbs in traditional light fixtures.

## SAD Lighting

If you find yourself having a hard time getting motivated and are experiencing sudden and significant mental issues, you may be suffering from Seasonal Affective Disorder (SAD). SAD is triggered by the altered natural light patterns created by a change in seasons (most commonly, fall to winter); symptoms may include depression, lack of energy, difficulty focusing, problems sleeping, negative thoughts, and more. Fortunately, there are both SAD lighting fixtures and full-spectrum SAD light bulbs on the market that are designed to spur a return to healthy circadian rhythms.

## Smart Storage

The right home office storage isn't just a matter of the physical furniture; it can also be affected by how you work. For instance, many offices—home and otherwise—continue to embrace a trend toward a paperless work environment. This isn't an all-or-nothing proposition. In some cases, it's about adopting certain practices that will cut down on the amount of paper you generate or interact with. For instance, many home office workers—and especially those who are self-employed—sign contracts electronically. Not only do they not have to print out paper versions, they save time by not having to scan or mail signed contracts. You can certainly go further than that by scanning any paper documents and storing them electronically. Most people, however, still deal with at least a modicum of paperwork. Much of that paper is important enough that it must be kept. That's where home office storage furniture comes in. The storage in any home office comes in two flavors: **open**, meaning whatever you store will be in plain view, and **concealed**. We'll discuss both here.

The shelves, drawers, and mini-closet combo in this guest bedroom easily convert into ample office storage space. If the owner ever abandons the office for a new job or even a new home, the unit can be converted to completely new storage needs, such as for seasonal linens or to accommodate a guest.

## Open storage

This translates to shelves. Shelving can be useful quick-access storage for supplies and reference sources such as dictionaries or technical manuals. It can be ideal for keeping office supplies accessible and for holding boxes containing anything you'll need to use in your work, or even boxed hanging files. The type of shelving you include can have a significant impact—both practically and aesthetically—on your home office.

**Standing bookshelves.** Whether you put them against a wall or use them as a room divider, freestanding bookshelves have a big footprint. When they're too large for the space, they can make a home office seem closed-in and confined, even claustrophobic. In the right place, though, a standing bookshelf can provide abundant usable storage in the form of an attractive piece of furniture. Tall standing bookshelves can also be effective room dividers to separate the home office from a larger space such as a living room. Standing bookshelves are excellent for framing one desk in a galley layout, or on either side of an isolated desk.

**Built-ins.** Built-in bookcases are a stunning addition to any interior design, but they add special flair and practical functionality to a home office. Optimize existing built-in units by positioning a desk or other work surface close enough to the shelves to have easy access whenever you might need it. A particularly effective look is to use a wall of built-in shelves as a backdrop to an isolated desk. This allows the home office professional to merely roll or reach back for books or other materials on the shelves and then turn around to work on the desk. If you're building in bookshelves from scratch as part of the process of creating your home office, it's wise to incorporate a desk between banks of shelves to create a visually blended, all-in-one structure.

The built-in storage blends seamlessly into this room.

This shed-based home office is kept neat and tidy thanks in part to standing bookshelves on either side of the desk.

**Wall-mounted shelves.** These include both bracket-supported shelving and floating shelves. In either case, there will be a limit to the weight the shelf can safely support. Thick, heavy reference works, for example, may tax the support structure of these shelves. Floating shelves are particularly prone to failure under a significant weight load. They are, however, some of the sleekest and most attractive shelves in any home office. Floating shelves are an excellent unobtrusive option placed right above a desk butted to a wall.

### Concealed storage

Paperless may not be the way you prefer to work. If that is the case, you'll need somewhere to organize and store the important paperwork your job produces. That inevitably means a file cabinet. Fortunately, you have many options beyond the tried-and-true steel blocks that have long defined many corporate offices. These days, upscale filing cabinets can make a design statement all by themselves. The looks and styles available rival what you might find among kitchen cabinets (that shouldn't come as a surprise, given that many of the manufacturers of home office file cabinet units also build kitchen cabinetry).

Your desk may come equipped with a hanging-file drawer, which may be all the file storage you need. If you need more, you can find freestanding cabinet units widely available in design styles ranging from traditional to modern. Ideally, though, select a file cabinet that matches or at least complements the desk you've chosen.

Wall-mounted shelves keep things out of the way but still accessible; having them high up like this reduces visual clutter while you focus on work.

A busy professional with a hectic business life and a multitude of storage needs can benefit from a mix of storage that includes hanging file drawers, traditional cabinets, open shelves, and drawers.

# Secure Storage

Safes are not a common addition to home offices, but if you work with sensitive and important documents, you may need to make sure information on paperwork or electronic storage devices can't be compromised or destroyed in a fire. A safe can offer a much higher level of protection than a locked desk drawer or file cabinet.

The most common home—and home office—safe is small but heavy. Safes are measured by interior capacity, and those for home use range from about 0.5 cubic feet (0.014 cubic meters) (appropriate for a collection of jewelry or a handgun) to more than 2 cubic feet (0.056 cubic meters). A 1.3-cubic-foot (0.037-cubic-meter) capacity will serve most home offices well. Although today's safes are fairly lightweight, look for one approaching 100 pounds (45kg). The heavier the unit, the more difficult it will be for a thief to cart it away. You should also keep an eye out for models tested by Underwriters Laboratories (UL). As with electrical equipment, the UL mark on a safe is a sign of integrity.

For maximum security, you can build a home office safe into a wall, although most people will opt for a freestanding safe kept in a cabinet. In any case, the best modern safes include a digital combination lock, multiple deadbolt bars, and a keyed override to use in case of power outage or in the event that the safe combination is lost.

## Fire

Fire-resistant safes will be clearly sold as such and will be rated to a high temperature. But that rating is only part of the story. You'll also need to check the rating for the internal temperature. If you're storing papers, you'll usually be fine with a safe rated for an internal temperature anywhere below 300°F (149°C). However, if you store photos, DVDs, CDs, flash drives, or external hard drives, look for a model rated not to exceed 125°F (52°C) internal temperature.

## Water

You would think that water protection would go hand in glove with fire resistance. However, you'd be wrong. Look for an explicit water resistance rating on the safe. This is even more important if your home is located in a floodplain or area that floods regularly. The rating will usually list the number of hours the safe will remain waterproof in a certain level of water.

## Theft

Keeping in mind that the safe is still keeping your valuables intact as long as it's not opened—even if it has been removed from your home—look for the "TL" rating. This is the UL test for resistance to common safe-breaking tools, like small explosives and drills. A TL-30 rating equals thirty minutes of endurance under assault.

## Features

The basic difference between inexpensive and middle- to high-end safes is keyed versus digital keypad. Digital keypads are convenient and usually come with override access keys in case you forget the combination or the primary lock simply quits working for whatever reason. Quality safes also have at least two and often three locking bolts. If you want to secure the safe in place, look for models with predrilled anchor holes or a safe that comes with a bolt-down kit.

## Specialized storage

Depending on the type of work you do, you may need to supplement your home office with specialized storage to suit your work. Builders, architects, and draftspeople will all need to add a flat-file cabinet for storing large blueprints or other oversized technical documents that should not be folded. These units are large, so they need to be planned into the layout from the start, not added as an afterthought. A seamstress or artist may benefit from a shelving unit of shallow cubbies to store a large variety of supplies close at hand. Don't forget specialty storage features when rounding out the home office design, because they may be difficult to shoehorn in later.

## All-in-one solutions

Computer armoires and hutches, as well as wall-mounted computer stations, can all supply a one-stop-shopping alternative to a suite of home office furniture. If you're okay with working in a confined space and don't require a lot of materials or electronic equipment in your work, one of these may be ideal for you. These are a way to save money and cut down on the time and effort of design and layout. Place or mount a single piece of furniture and you're ready to go. Many of these options have internal cable and cord channels that make connecting your equipment a breeze—not to mention organizing what can otherwise be annoying visual clutter. A key benefit of an armoire, hutch, or wall-mounted workstation is the fact that at the end of the day, you can shut the lid or doors and create a physical separation from your work. These are also wonderful options for small apartments or in a situation where you need to fit a home office into an existing bedroom or other small, cluttered space. Although the workspace can be rather tight, as long as you're organized, everything will be within easy reach.

Wall-mounted desks are natural space-savers. Many, like this one, are meant to be paired with companion storage spaces that create a wall-mounted "suite" to accommodate work files and office supplies. These type of prefab creations are inexpensive, easy to install, and available in different wood tones and several different design styles.

# Screens and Dividers

Create greater separation between a home office and a larger room or space by introducing a partition. A movable screen or even a less-portable room divider can visually isolate a home office, dull sound transmission into and out of the workspace, and foster greater focus on work-related matters.

## Screens

Folding screens are some of the most elementary of home office partitions. They are more about blocking sight lines than muting sound, but they are fairly inexpensive options to introduce a strong separation. They can also be a style accent. Choose from upholstered screens, solid wood versions, or framed plastic or glass panels. Each creates its own distinctive look, so revisit the design style that you're trying to establish for the workspace and let that guide your decision (as well as, obviously, the constraints of budget).

Screens are generally defined by the number of panels, ranging from one and going up to six or more. Three-panel screens are the most common because they offer a great deal of concealment but are still easy enough for one person to move, fold, and unfold (and they naturally have better balance than screens of one or two panels). You'll also have to decide if you want full-length (solid from floor to top of screen) or more traditional footed panels. Full-length panels provide slightly more privacy and quiet. Beyond those preliminary choices, you'll pick a screen that answers your design brief and goals for the space and your home at large. Acoustic panel screens absorb significantly more sound and are a good choice for a busy, loud household. It's wise to pick a screen that could feasibly be repurposed elsewhere in the house if you return to work in a formal office or change jobs.

If concealment is your primary goal, choose a screen that blends with the space and color scheme of the larger room. Here, an apartment's tiny home office is concealed behind a screen that has been painted the same color as the wall. Although it is an unconventional treatment, it effectively hides the office without calling attention to itself.

A ceiling-mounted divider such as this open design can be an effective visual divider for a space like this while still leaving the open and airy feeling intact. To block sound, however, the divider would need to be solid.

## Dividers

All screens are dividers, but not all dividers are screens. Dividers are, in fact, built with openings that allow air and light to pass through. They can maintain an open and airy feeling while establishing borders between the home office and everywhere else. One of the most common home office dividers is a two-sided bookcase. Filled with books or storage boxes, it creates a custom wall. If you leave some openings unfilled, you maintain a view through the divider that allows you to see what's happening in the rest of the room or the house. That's also a way to allow light and air to penetrate both sides of the divider.

Ceiling-mounted curtains are a less common option, but they can be a unique visual statement in the right room. Tracks are fastened to the ceiling and the curtain is hung directly from the track or from a pole fixed to the track. Tracks can be straight-line or curved, and they are available in several different finishes. The curtains themselves can be crafted to suit, opening up a wide range of possibilities. Choose based on how much privacy and light transmission you need.

You can also get decorative with a room divider, using the opportunity to add a powerful design element. A row of lush, tall-growing potted houseplants would make a unique living screen. Painted cinderblocks, steel slats, recycled pallets, and more can be pressed into service as one-of-a-kind dividers. Custom options include anything that can reasonably hang from the ceiling or be secured between ceiling and floor.

# Rugs and Protective Mats

Let's be realistic: in most home offices, the floor that's there is the flooring you have to work with. Swapping out the flooring in one corner of the living room or even in a guest bedroom is likely to be too expensive to even consider when creating a home office. That doesn't mean that you have to live with what's underfoot; it just means you have to be creative.

## Carpet

The soft bounce and pleasant feel of a carpeted floor is a big plus for any space where you're spending the better part of your day. Add to that the sound-deadening properties of carpeting and the fact that it maintains warmth in colder months, and it's an obvious choice for any home office. If you prefer something harder or firmer under your work area, you can turn to a bamboo or semi-rigid area rug like sisal. Yes, it's a totally legitimate interior design technique to place one rug on top of another. You may even come to love the look.

Even if you aren't putting anything on top of the carpet, use an office mat under your chair to reduce the wear and tear on the carpet. The least expensive versions are clear vinyl or polycarbonate and will stand up to years of a rolling office chair and traffic to and from your desk, leaving the carpet underneath relatively pristine.

A carpeted room is a luxury for a home office. Given the traffic and use a home office carpet will see, however, the best choice is a low-pile, high-quality, durable option such as the Berber carpet in this sophisticated and classic workspace.

## Flooring in unfinished spaces

If you're starting from scratch to create a home office in a utility space or outbuilding, your choice of flooring will only be limited by budget. Start by eliminating the less-than-perfect options. Although wood flooring is beautiful, it tends to be pricier than a home workspace justifies. The involved installation process only increases that cost. Stone and ceramic tile are also not ideal for a home office. Hard surfaces create a lot of bounce-around noise in a space where quiet is at a premium and may even be a necessity. Hard surfaces are also a little rougher on your feet and legs, especially if you'll be walking on them all day, every day. So, even in hotter areas of the country and where it might match other floors in the home, hard tile is generally not a good idea for a home office.

Softer surfaces, on the other hand, can inject comfort into your workday. King among these is carpeting. The better quality the carpeting and pad are, the softer and more luxurious the feel under your feet. Although premium carpet can be expensive, in the small square footage of most utility spaces or outbuildings, even high-quality carpeting probably won't break the bank. Avoid bargain carpet because, given how much you'll be using a home office, cheap carpet will probably wear quickly and look dingy in short order.

Resilient (the industry term for soft) flooring is also a good choice for a home office. This type comes in sheets, planks, or tiles and is usually incredibly easy to install—even for the inexperienced home DIYer. You should be able to install a resilient plank or tile floor in a day. This category of floor includes inexpensive vinyl, laminates, and linoleum or Marmoleum. All come in easy-to-assemble, click-together planks or tiles in convincing looks that mimic a variety of stone and wood surfaces. Vinyl and linoleum are also available as sheet products, although the two are very different. Linoleum is a natural product with antibacterial and antimicrobial properties; vinyl is a synthetic that can off-gas volatile organic compounds (VOCs) but is far less expensive. Both are amazingly durable.

No matter what surface you choose as the foundation for your office—or what surface is already there—invest in a chair mat. Whether you're using a rolling chair or a version with legs, you'll be moving it so often that damaging the floor over time is almost a guarantee without some sort of floor protection. The wide range of chair mats means that you can choose from inexpensive versions that are largely invisible or opt for a pricier option that lets you inject color and pattern into your home office.

This visual artist's workspace illustrates the possibilities of putting your home office in a shed. Although this is a prefab shed sold by a shed company, the structure as sold leaves a lot of room for fabrication and personalization. The eye-catching color is tempered by a pickled laminate floor that is beautiful in its own right. It is also durable, and paint or other spills will be easier to clean up than if the owner had chosen carpet.

# Working Wall Space

Home offices are typically space-challenged. Using all available surfaces as efficiently as possible is key to making a comfortable workspace and being super productive in that space. The often-overlooked asset in pursuit of that goal is vertical surfaces. In short, open wall space is mighty valuable real estate.

## Work boards

The obvious candidate for wall mounting is a corkboard or a whiteboard. The choice is a matter of how you work. If you do a lot of "blue sky" brainstorming, especially if you include colleagues in your think sessions, a whiteboard might be an invaluable addition to your home office. A stylized alternative that might fit better into the overall home design is a large square painted with chalkboard paint. A corkboard or bulletin board will prove more useful for anyone with a lot of documents, charts, tables, or other reference materials that need to be kept at a glance. Pinning them up will make them much more available than they would be in a pile on your desk. If either of these options looks too utilitarian for your particular design sense, you can easily put together a decorative frame that will soften the look a bit. Any frame store can cut the pieces for you if you provide them with the outside measurements of the board.

## Wall-mounted shelves and cabinets

Of course, wall surfaces aren't just good for board mounting. Wall-mounted shelves or cabinets can be incredibly useful to store items, anything from extra office supplies to a printer that has nowhere else to sit. Shelves can also be a design accent, because wall-mounted versions are available in the full spectrum of interior design styles—from rustic farmhouse to sleek modern. That means that shelves can be useful for bridging the divide between the look of the larger space and the look of the home office area.

A wall-mounted cabinet is an incredibly useful addition to any home office, but it is particularly effective in a smaller workspace with little square footage on which to place traditional standing shelves or freestanding storage. This unit is a little handier than most thanks to cubbies on either end that allow the worker to store frequently used materials in easy-access openings.

# CHOOSING COLORS AND PATTERNS

Color is one of the most commonly disregarded elements in home office design. The focus is so tight on function that it is easy to overlook adding a pleasing—much less intriguing—look. But there are practical reasons for carefully choosing a home office color. Color in any space where we spend a lot of time inevitably has an effect on how tired we get, how much energy we'll have during the day, and how enjoyable we find the space. Happily, color is an easy design element to inject into any home office.

Dark blue, with its connotations of authority and professionalism, is an ideal color for this stately home office positioned along one entire living room wall. The stunning cabinetry provides ample storage as well as being an unforgettable design statement. Dark, dramatic colors like this aren't for every home office or home-based worker, but in the right space, they can be incredibly powerful and dynamic.

# Color Moods, Emotions, and Associations

The colors we live with can have a profound effect on our moods and psychological outlook. Here is a condensed list of the qualities associated with different colors. The shades of these colors—such as purple or royal blue—have similar connotations. Keep in mind that when talking about a color such as black or deep purple, the idea is not to cover the room in the color. Shades such as charcoal or violet used sparingly may fully achieve the color's mood.

| Color | Mood | Perceived Associations | Home Office Role |
|-------|------|------------------------|------------------|
| Blue | Safe | Security, strength, authority | Focus for quiet tasks, great for accounting |
| Purple | Playful | Royalty, luxury, dignity | Thoughtful, excellent for executive coach |
| Green | Calm | Nature, life, growth | Balanced, natural for financial professional |
| Red | Passionate | Love, danger, excitement | High energy, works for salesperson |
| Orange | Impulsive | Fun, warmth, wealth | Nurturing, great for pro home consultant |
| Yellow | Happy | Energy, friendliness | Positive, good for a designer |
| Beige | Neutral | Neutrality, convention, calm | Versatile, fosters a range of work tasks |
| White | Fresh | Cleanliness, purity, goodness | Clean, orderly environment for writer or editor |
| Black | Somber | Strength, drama, seriousness | Impressive, good for lawyer or business owner |

Whether you know it or not, your eye reads a lot into the color of a room. For instance, studies have shown that the color red can actually quicken a person's pulse. Certain colors may be difficult to look at over long periods of time. What's more, the combination of colors you use can amplify the effect of any one color. We also subconsciously associate colors with certain values. There's a reason why new brides wear white, with its associations of purity, and why so many lipstick shades are versions of passionate red. Of course, personal preference should play a part in color choice; everybody has his or her own favorite hue.

Beyond those intangibles, there are practical aspects to colors. Lighter shades, neutrals, and whites are easier to keep clean because dirt shows more readily. Darker colors absorb and hold heat during the day and can noticeably increase the physical temperature in a room. The property of any color is also radically affected by the surface finish through which the eye detects the color. Shiny surfaces and gloss paint reflect a maximum amount of light and can create hot spots in our field of view, or glare on a computer monitor. Matte surfaces can dull a color and show fingerprints. Eggshell or satin finishes split the difference between those two extremes, which is why they are the most common finishes in home offices.

Gray is soothing, sophisticated, and professional. All that makes it a wonderful color for a home-based workspace. Slightly darker grays don't show dirt as readily as neutral hues might, and a color like the one in this shed-based home office will seem fresh and pleasing for a long time to come. It's an easy shade to live and work with. The exterior of the shed is painted a lighter shade of gray, coordinating the color scheme and making this particular home office an excellent place to meet colleagues or clients.

## Strategies for integrating home office color

**1. Blend.** When choosing a dominant color or color scheme for your home office, keep in mind how it reads in the larger space. In many cases, as with a kitchen-based workspace or a home office in the corner of a living room or master bedroom, painting walls to accommodate the home office might create a jarring visual contrast. But even in a whole-room home office, using a color scheme or individual colors that clash with the design of the house will create too much separation and can even detract from home value.

**2. Adapt.** Regardless of what space your home office occupies, you can use visual clues to define the home office area while complementing adjacent and attached spaces. Wall art is a handy tool for this. Art is a wonderful choice because it can be swapped out to revitalize the look, and you can also easily try out different appearances to see what suits your workday best. When choosing office furnishings, move beyond the institutional black, brown, beige, or white in picking your filing cabinets, chair, and even desk. For instance, a sunflower yellow office chair would be a dynamite, eye-pleasing addition to the home office and would complement a light brown sofa or sage green easy chair in the room.

**3. Accent.** You can easily achieve a strong color statement that does not detract from the home's overall interior design through the use of accents. That includes rugs and rolling chair pads, wall tapestries for soundproofing, divider screens (which can be upholstered, colored glass, painted wood, or even painted metal), and desk blotters—available in many different colors.

Perhaps the easiest way to blend a home office into a larger space is to leave the wall and trim colors the same. The colors of the lamp, desktop, and chair are all natural and subdued; the overall feeling established by the wall color is one of freshness and simplicity.

The home office area in the open floor plan of this apartment is marked by bright black-and-white photos that pop against the dark gray background of the wall. This is an excellent and distinctive way to indicate a work area in a larger space, and the effect would work just as well with art in contrasting or complementary colors.

## Patterns

Pattern is cousin to color in interior design. Carefully including a pattern or patterns in your home office can add visual interest and boost the energy of the space. "Carefully" is the watchword. Loud, busy patterns can add energy but also create jarring visual noise that can be distracting. That's why it's always good to start by introducing one simple, two-tone pattern. Something like a checkerboard area rug under your desk and chair can be ideal. Play with more adventurous patterns as you get more comfortable working in your office. You can also use pattern to integrate the home office more fully into the home at large by repeating common patterns used in different rooms throughout the house.

Pattern doesn't have to be in your face to be effective in a home office. The lines in the rug and the ceiling of this space contrast the circular clocks on the wall, creating an interesting and engaging visual tension that adds some upbeat energy to the workspace. Pattern is often used to add a little jolt to a room, and that's no different in a home office.

# PERSONALIZATION

One of the wonderful things about a home office is that you can make it all your own, in a way that you can't when working in an on-site office. Obviously, you'll need to show some restraint in accessorizing a workplace where you will host colleagues or even clients. But if you're going to be working alone all the time, you should personalize the space to create a work environment that you'll enjoy every minute you're there.

## Plants

Houseplants are excellent additions to any home office. They can add eye-pleasing color and form, softening the workspace and making it homier. Most houseplants require little care beyond the occasional watering, and several actually improve the air in a home office (see the sidebar below). Indoor houseplant pots and containers are an additional opportunity to add design accents to your work area.

## Five Great Air-Purifying Home Office Plants

Be aware that even though an indoor houseplant—just like its outdoor cousins—takes in carbon dioxide and expels oxygen, it's not a replacement for a local or whole-house air filtration unit. However, some species are actually fairly effective at screening out toxins in the air. Their benefit will be amplified by using more than one plant in the space. In any case, these all also add visually lovely accents. As with most houseplants, the air-purifying favorites below are low maintenance and shade tolerant. They will usually do well regardless of the sun exposure your home office receives.

Spider plant

Cornstalk dracaena

Boston fern

Bamboo palm

Ficus tree

## Decoration

Don't let decoration be an afterthought in the process of creating your home office. After all, the ability to endlessly customize your workspace is a key difference between a home office and a workspace in an office building. It's an easy equation. Decorating is all about personalizing the space. The more personal it is, the more comfortable the space will be. The more comfortable you are at work, the more productive you will be. Start with cues from the rest of the house. You'll better integrate the home office into your general interior design by repeating specific colors, textures, or objects from other rooms in the house. For instance, something as simple as cabinet knobs, matching light fixtures, or photo frames can visually tie the home office to your overall interior design.

Textiles are excellent home office accents because they soften the look of what can sometimes be an overly utilitarian space, adding both texture and color (and possibly pattern). A throw draped over the back of your office chair, simple curtains or drapes in a sumptuous fabric, or a fabric wall hanging can all be a way to make the space your own while visually warming it up.

Art is an obvious way to personalize the look and feel of your home office. The right art in the right place can impact the mood and nature of the space, which is something to keep in mind when choosing what you'll put up on the walls or sit on a desk or shelves. Any art should be visually interesting so that you don't grow bored with it. However, if you regularly have visitors to your home office, edit your art. Avoid anything that might be considered controversial or is overly personal. Remember, it's important to project professionalism; otherwise, you risk not being taken seriously. You should also choose whatever art you include based on the nature of the space and the work you do. High-energy, bold-colored art might be right for a designer, while something more sedate, calming, and meditative would be more appropriate for a bookkeeper's office or an editor's workspace. The point is, in all cases, to think through the impact the artwork will have on the space.

Even hardware can be a design accent. Here, a mounting arm, used to add flexiblity in the use of the computer monitor, actually complements the look of the home office, echoing the desk legs, keyboard, and mouse. A chrome or metal arm would not have been as complementary to the other elements in the space.

The framed art over this home office desk adds visual interest to the space and provides some relief in the largely white space. Splashes of color do their part, too, and complement touches of the same color in the art.

# CHAPTER 3

# BETTER WAYS TO WORK FROM HOME

Once you have your home office set up, the job is not quite done. Working from home is a continuous process of adjusting expectations and making sure your workday works for you. You'll need to put in time and effort to make sure you're working efficiently and professionally, as well as taking advantage of all possible aspects of working from home and nipping potential problems in the bud. It's all covered in this chapter.

Successfully working from home means paying attention to many aspects of technology and work/life balance—all covered in this chapter.

# WORK-FROM-HOME TIPS

If you haven't worked from home before, getting into a productive groove can be a challenge. Maintaining your productivity as the novelty of working from home wears off is even more of a challenge. Your physical workspace will have a big impact on that.
The bigger trick, though, will be balancing the discipline you need to get your work done against keeping your home a place to relax and enjoy your life away from work. It's far too easy to blur those lines. Your success is going to lie in your day-to-day  practices. Follow the time-tested guidelines here and you'll be productive in your home office *and* fully enjoy your home after the workday is over.

## Schedule

A lack of structure has tripped up many a work-at-home professional. Set a schedule. Yes, sometimes work and life can throw you curves and the schedule will need to change, but make sure you have one to begin with. It doesn't matter if you want to work irregular or odd hours; you can still  schedule those hours. Neglect to do that and you're certain to eventually slide into time-wasting habits that burn through precious workday hours.

## Routines

Okay, you're not a robot. But routines give the day structure and are our signals to ourselves of what comes next. Having breakfast at the same time every morning can be a way to commence your workday like a starting gun begins a race. Getting into a routine for checking emails or social media only at particular points during the day—rather than on a haphazard, continual basis—will help you focus on your work without distractions. Check the Resources on page 124 for programs that can help you block distractions during the workday.

## Dress for success

What you wear is a subtle reinforcement of what activity you'll be undertaking. If you wear pajamas to work, you're telling yourself that you should be sleeping or relaxing. While you're working for a living, dress like it.

## Exploit apps

There is a wealth of software available to help you make the most of working at home. Time-tracking apps, for instance, ensure you don't waste half the day on social media. Schedule-management programs, file managers, cloud-based backups, and other applications will save you time and energy and keep you focused on work and the bottom line. (For a sampling of these apps and programs, see page 120.)

## Take breaks

Scheduled, regular breaks are as important at home as they are in a corporate workplace. You need to regularly get away from your screen, walk around, and take a break from work so that you can stay fresh for the entire workday. A good  rule of thumb is to take a short break of ten or twenty minutes per hour of screen time.

## Interact regularly

It doesn't matter if it's the delivery person, a local coffee shop pickup, or a video chat with coworkers: social interaction is key to thriving in a home office. Isolation is a problem with many work-at-home workers, and it's a problem that can sneak up on you in surprising ways—such as in the form of depression and job dissatisfaction.

# BETTER VIDEO MEETINGS

People commonly use laptops for videoconferencing, but most models are less than ideal. The size of most laptop screens does not allow you to effectively see detail and participants clearly in larger group meetings, and the built-in cameras are not high quality. Use a desktop or all-in-one if possible—or use the workarounds described in this section.

Video meetings from your home office are fast becoming the norm, if they aren't already the norm in your personal work life. Fortunately, several companies have developed easy-to-use software that allows even large groups to meet and interact online. The problem is, technological progress has outstripped the development of commonsense rules for participating in videoconferences and meetings. This section is focused on offering that guidance.

The main issues you have to consider before you can maximize the potential of business videoconferencing are lighting, sound, and picture quality. There are levels to each of these, from basic workability through advanced video and audio effects. The difference usually has to do with the sophistication of the equipment you're using—which translates to expense. You'll have to decide what's reasonable based on your needs or budget; a few monthly meetings held with colleagues might not require a great deal of sophistication and polish. On the other hand, if you regularly pitch to potential clients or board members, you may find it well worth your while to upgrade to a high-end lighting rig, camera, and microphone.

**Lighting** is often the most misunderstood element in videoconferencing. Although it won't affect the technical aspects of a video meeting, it has an enormous impact on how you will be perceived. A good way to start out is to use only natural light or artificial light, but not a combination. If you're using natural light for the video meeting, no window should be directly behind you (even if you have blinds or curtains); this can easily create a silhouette or annoying hot spots in your image. Windows should ideally be behind the camera and slightly off to the side. Obviously, you can't move windows in your home office, so artificial lighting is going to be more adaptable to your videoconferencing needs.

This is great natural lighting for a video call: the bright natural light is a suitable distance away and facing toward but not directly shining on the worker.

If you only have one office lamp, shine it on your face from behind the camera and off to the side. You'll get an even better effect by bouncing the light off a nearby wall onto your face. Professional photographers usually light their subjects with "scrim" lighting—fixtures covered with opaque, light-diffusing screens. You can use the same trick by covering your lamps with white vellum or a similar white material (as long as it's not flammable). The idea is to avoid skin highlights, hot spots, and shadows.

If you're regularly giving video presentations or having online meetings with important clients, you may want to invest in a three-point web video lighting setup. The typical setup includes LED panel lights with diffusing screens and brackets or clamps that allow the lights to be mounted to a desk. Many of these lights are USB-compatible and can be controlled from your computer or smartphone.

**Sound control** goes hand-in-hand with effective lighting. If you're going to participate in a video meeting or conference, you need to hear and be heard. At the most basic level, you can use your computer's built-in microphone. Depending on the acoustics in your home office and the quality of your computer, the audio from the internal mic will range from "barely acceptable" to "okay." It's almost never ideal.

Spend just a little money and you can get a decent USB microphone that plugs into your computer and makes your voice appreciably clearer during a videoconference. A directional mic is even better, because you can point it right at your mouth. A lavalier microphone is a clip-on version that puts the mic close to your mouth. These are easy to use, nearly invisible on screen, and come in wired or wireless versions.

The more expensive the microphone, the more options you'll have for adjusting sound levels to create crisp, precise sound during the videoconference. At the very least, you'll want a microphone with decent noise-cancelling properties. Although our ears at good at filtering out background noises, videoconferencing software is not.

You may be amazed to find out just how distracting the dishwasher or fan running nearby can be.

The other side of the sound coin is what you hear. You can work with your computer's speakers, but that's generally not going to cut it, so headphones are recommended. In many cases, your ear will catch more details if you use earbuds or headphones. Although they don't look as natural on camera, either of these also contains the sound of the videoconference—a plus if you don't want to disturb anyone else in the house or if the meeting will cover sensitive information that others shouldn't hear. Earbuds are fine for the occasional video interaction, but if your video meetings run long or you participate in a lot of them, headphones will be more comfortable.

Your **camera** is the third part of the home office videoconferencing equation. Higher-end and newer computers include reasonably good built-in cameras. Laptop cameras and those in older computers are generally a bit low quality for effective or frequent videoconferencing. The good news is that upgrading to a basic HD external webcam is not a significant expense.

Because earbuds are so ubiquitous these days, it's likely that you have a pair and can use them for videoconferencing. They provide better sound transmission than computer speakers, allowing you to hear other people in the meeting more clearly. They are also less visually intrusive than headphones.

There are great many to choose from, but all are fairly compact, easy to connect and use, and clip right onto your computer screen. The most common resolution for these cameras is high definition at this point, but whether the final image is truly hi-def will depend on a number of factors, including your computer's video capabilities, the videoconferencing software and settings you use, and the speed of your broadband connection.

## Three Quick Checks before Starting a Video Meeting

**1. Preview and declutter.** Before you start the video call, boot up your camera and look behind you. Everything in the frame will be seen by other people on the call. It's easy to overlook that dirty towel draped over the door, and a whole bunch of tchotchkes can look unprofessional. An easy way to ensure you avoid this at all times is to automatically use the "blur" feature available in some video chat programs, which blurs out what's behind you. But don't rely on it to cover up something truly unprofessional.

**2. Limit motion.** You'll make it a lot easier for others on the video to watch you when you speak if there is nothing else moving in the frame, like a pet or traffic in a window. Try to limit your own movement as well, especially if you are sitting in a rolling desk chair—lock the wheels before the meeting starts if you can.

**3. Know the software.** Fumbling to find the mute-unmute tab or button can be a meeting killer, especially if you keep accidentally muting yourself or blacking out your image. Make sure you're familiar with how the software works; most have tutorials on their websites.

## Ideal Video Protocol

The protocol for any work-related videoconference depends in part on the people participating in the conference (informal gathering of colleagues, or direct reports speaking with upper management). But there are general commonsense guidelines that can help any videoconference go more smoothly and head off any potential faux pas.

**Prepare.** It's wise to have a snack before going on camera. It can be a bit shocking how much a microphone can pick up, including the embarrassing grumbling of an empty stomach. Have a glass of water off camera in case your mouth gets dry. Collect any paperwork you might need before the meeting, so you don't become a blurry chaotic image trying to find something you're referencing. Close other applications and programs that may compete with the videoconferencing software for computer resources and especially upload bandwidth. Shared bandwidth is one of the most common reasons for choppy video.

**Set your distance and height.** Sit too close to the camera and your video image will be oversized—all head and nothing else. Too far away and you look lost in the frame. Ideally, sit just far away enough from the camera so that the image captured includes the bottom of your chest to the top of your head. Don't lean toward or away from the camera during the meeting. The height of your chair should put the camera at eye level so that it appears you're looking directly at the other videoconference participants.

**Dress for success.** What you wear can have a huge impact on how you look during a videoconference. Avoid any reflective jewelry, which can create distracting and irritating hot spots. Avoid fine patterns on your clothing, because some may create moiré patterns that visually vibrate while your image is onscreen. Light, solid colors are preferable to black or very dark colors, or white.

**Be cautious with screen sharing.** Screen sharing allows you to show work on your desktop, such as an open spreadsheet or graphic file, to the other videoconferencing participants. It can be incredibly useful for working collaboratively on projects. Just keep in mind that the

Dress professionally for a video call, but also with a mind to successful video streaming—no overly intricate patterns or light-catching jewelry. This worker has the right idea.

entire screen is visible, not just the file you're working on and showing to the group. If you have an odd, personal desktop background, or have used quirky folder names for folders on your desktop, those will show up in the screen share—clean them up.

**Use chat sparingly.** Most modern videoconferencing software includes an onscreen chat feature where you can type thoughts while others are speaking. If there are a lot of people in the meeting and several are using the chat feature, it can detract from what speakers are saying and become a form of annoying side chatter. Only use it when it's essential—such as alerting the session moderator that your video is cutting out.

## Creating a Special Videoconferencing Space

With all of the guidance we've discussed so far in mind, you may want to consider setting up a separate, distinct area or backdrop that you use for all video calls. It can be difficult to have everything just right for video calls when you're already designing your home office to fulfill so many other needs. If you have a laptop, you can simply carry the laptop to your ideal video space and have the call, then return to your normal home office. If your computer is stationary but the background less than ideal, you can create a temporary background that will improve the situation.

A room divider screen can make a perfect backdrop that's easy to whip out and then tuck away again—or utilize in a room—as needed.

Full bookshelves that are far away enough not to distract the viewer are a good choice for a backdrop.

For a temporary backdrop, purchase a large sheet of foam board, a very wide bulletin board, or some other stiff, large surface with which to work. Customize it however you like, whether that's painting it one color that will work well on camera (not too dark, not too light) or covering it with fabric. Use it to block the unsightly view of an incorrigibly messy bookshelf or hang it to cover an unfortunately located utility box. Alternatively, you could install a curtain rod out of frame behind your work area and draw the curtains on whatever it is you wish to hide.

If you can move your laptop to a new location for a call, you can get really creative with whatever small slice of your home will serve your needs the best. Is there underused shelving in a corner of a large living room? Repurpose it with some tasteful and carefully placed home décor items that give a little life to your background without distracting from you as a speaker. Is the lighting in your kitchen perfect and the cabinetry new and beautiful? Declutter a small area of countertop behind your temporary call spot and use the area to your advantage. If you're limited on space but really need a good background, keep a "reset" box of decorative items that you whip out for calls but put away when done so that the space can return to its other uses.

## Recording Video Meetings

There are several good reasons for recording a video meeting. First, replaying a videoconference can allow you to improve how you conduct yourself in one—you can review and critique your own performance. It's also your chance to check the technical aspect of the session, verifying that your video wasn't choppy and that your audio was clear. You can use a recording to double-check any action items that were discussed in a long meeting, ensuring nothing falls through the cracks, or to create summary notes. If the videoconference includes clients or outside contractors, a recording may provide legal protections if something goes amiss in the future.

There are restrictions to consider. Always be transparent: let others know they are being recorded. This may even be a legal requirement. Check if the companies and clients involved allow or have rules dictating video recording. If proprietary information is going to be discussed, you'll probably need explicit permission to record. In any case, it's your ethical responsibility to handle the video recording file with discretion and care.

# WORKING FROM HOME WITH KIDS

The exceptional circumstances of a global pandemic have added even more stress than normal into the lives of work-from-home parents. It's hard enough to discipline yourself to work efficiently in a home office in the best of times. But when children are forced to stay at home and away from group activities, that only compounds the challenge. The challenge increases the more children you have, and the younger they are.

Managing your children's time and energy alongside your work-at-home requirements starts with honesty. If your child or children are old enough to understand, it's imperative to have a straightforward talk with them.

Working in your home office while you have young children at home is a matter of balance and keeping calm while you juggle often competing demands.

Lay out why you're working from home and what that means. Explain that this isn't an optional activity; it's how you earn a living to buy things that the family needs, like food, clothing, and the house itself. It will help if you can tie this discussion as much as possible to the child's world. Mention that part of the money you'll earn from what you do in a home office will go toward toys and vacations. Tell your kids that sometimes they will have to act as if they are in an office building rather than in their home. That's their "part" in the process. Give them that responsibility and they may well surprise you by how completely they embrace their roles and rise to the occasion.

Also understand that children learn best through repetition and reinforcement. You may have to repeat instructions or directions and deal with some unintentional breaking of the rules. Stay cool; this time is as unusual for your children as it is for you. The best gift you can possibly give them is patience. Go over rules and guidelines for behavior as often as necessary until your children adopt them as habits.

You'll also have to be aware that children of different ages require different strategies. You may be able to schedule your grade-schooler's day to avoid having him barge into your home office at all, while it might work better to set aside time with your teen to ensure she doesn't feel neglected and to talk over issues of concern to her.

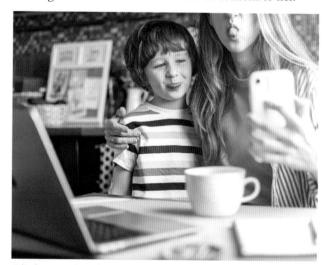

A little attention during your workday can go a long way. Sometimes all children need is to share a fun moment with you and know you are there for them before they go back off to amuse themselves for the next few hours.

## Kid-Friendly Rules for Home Office Time

Setting down some basic guidelines for the little (or even not-so-little) ones will make balancing the needs of your family and your time in your home office much easier. Children can't be expected to know what to do unless they're directed to right and wrong behaviors.

**1. Power words.** Rather than finding yourself screaming at your children as their shouting match interrupts your important business video meeting, agree on code words that require actions. Instruct the kids, "When I say X, quiet down and turn off the TV." Ask them if they understand, and then do a test run during the workweek. You can have words for noisy behavior, for when a child needs to leave the home office, and other situations. Power words are great shortcuts and can save you an angry outburst and spare children hurt feelings.

**2. Access.** Children need to know when they are allowed in your home office space, even if the office is part of a larger room. Set guidelines; these can be based on time, situations, or both. If children don't have rules regarding access, they'll likely intrude on your home office at the most inconvenient times. That won't serve the children's needs or help your stress level.

**3. Perfect a points system.** Okay, you can call it bribing. But used in moderation, this can be an effective behavior-modification technique, one that will enable you to maintain your sanity while you make your living. It's a simple system: If the children honor workday and home office rules, they accrue points. The points can be used for something like a pizza and root beer float on Friday night (with video games!) or other prizes. You have to be careful not to go overboard, but this can be a positive, upbeat, and fun solution to ensuring children behave when you're focused on work. It's the carrot as opposed to the stick.

## Adapting the Home Office for Children

In addition to helping your kids adapt to professional work being done in their home environment, you can also adapt the home office to accommodate your children to one degree or another. The simplest, most basic way to do this is to have a "fun" box in the room for young children. Fill it with all kinds of dollar-store surprises—inexpensive toys and craft supplies that will spur a child's imagination and keep him or her occupied while you work. Coloring books with crayons or colored pencils, molding clay or putty, crepe paper and child-proof scissors, and vellum sheets, sketchpads, and markers are all good choices for the box. Make sure you set the rule that whoever pulls something out of the box has to put it back in the box before he or she leaves the room. Entice your child by adding a new, fun object each week.

Adapting the home office space for older grade-schoolers, tweens, and young teens requires a slightly different tack. If your job does not require a lot of direct contact with clients or colleagues—either in person or by video—you might want to add workstations for older kids right in the home office. Those can be serious spaces where a child can work on homework, personal projects, journaling, or other quiet pursuits. It's a way to have your cake and eat it too, because you'll be working while you spend time with your kids. As a bonus, you'll also be able to more closely monitor homework assignments and class projects, and you can check your child's work in progress.

But managing children and the requirements of the home office isn't only about the children. Be straight up with bosses, colleagues, clients, and vendors. There is no sense in hiding or diminishing the fact that you're a parent with parental responsibilities. Remember that a great number of your coworkers are in the same boat. Make it clear to everyone that you may need to occasionally miss or reschedule meetings because of childcare duties. Once other professionals understand that you're working around

A wonderful solution to dealing with older grade-schoolers and beyond is to add workstations to your home office so that your children can do homework, work on craft projects, or simply read next to you while you work. It's a great way to put in your work hours and keep an eye on them at the same time.

a child or children's schedule, they are usually flexible in how they work with you. But they'll be less so if they have no idea why you keep rescheduling meetings.

Juggling children and working at home may require that you exploit your available resources. Maybe you have to tap Grandma and Grandpa to take your daughter one day a week so that you can tackle videoconferencing or in-depth paperwork. Negotiate with your partner or spouse to alternate childcare responsibilities and free up available time in the home office in large, uninterrupted blocks. Of course, a high-pressure job that requires your undivided attention and sucks up long hours during the day may mean hiring a professional, ranging from an experienced babysitter to a full-time nanny. Whatever help you require, you won't get it until you recognize the need and take steps to ask for or hire that help.

A few miscellaneous specific changes may help you work more efficiently, with less irritation and interruption. Sound-deadening strategies will make life more pleasant for any home office worker who is dealing with kids in the home; read all about your options on page 37. The issue of sound produced by your children may even influence

where you decide to put the home office. You should also secure your work computer with password protection, because you don't want kids being tempted to investigate if Mom or Dad's computer is more fun than their game console.

Working side by side—or, more likely, you working while your child entertains him- or herself—can allow for quiet chill time together. Try working together for an hour at the kitchen table, then returning to your home office for necessary private work time.

# TAX ADVANTAGES

One of the rewards of working at home is the potential to take a tax deduction for a dedicated home office space. Depending on your tax situation, other deductions you'll be taking, and the size and scope of your home office, that benefit can be significant. The guidelines that follow are a summary of the general requirements and limitations drawn from the 2019 tax year. However, keep in mind that the tax code regularly changes. That's why you should always consult your accountant or tax professional, or the IRS directly, when incorporating a working office into your home.

## Exclusive use

A central factor in whether you can deduct the home office space or not is "exclusive" and "regular" use. This means the home office is your principal place of business. The obvious part of this is that you use the space full-time for your occupation. The less obvious point—and something that can disqualify the deduction—is sole use. If your spouse takes over the space one night each week to pay bills, or you use it to indulge in a hobby on your off-hours, there's a chance you won't be able to take the home office deduction.

## Separation

The deduction is made much clearer when the home office is entirely separated from the rest of the home, but in most cases, a clear division qualifies the space. Something as simple as a room divider or freestanding bookshelves can fulfill the requirement.

## Primary business

The home office must be used for your principal occupation and means of earning an income. Even if you are a highly successful amateur stock trader and use the office to make significant supplementary revenue, you likely won't qualify for the deduction. The same is true for the teacher, bank employee, or insurance professional who makes a few bucks by using the office to sell crafts through an online platform on evenings and weekends.

## Percentage

So, if you meet the criteria, what type of deduction will you get? That is (as of 2019) a function of how large the office is in respect to the size of the house. For the sake of an example, let's say your office—including desk, storage, and work area—encompasses 100 square feet, and your house is 1,000 square feet. Your "business percentage" for the purposes of deduction will be 10 percent (100 ÷ 1000 = 10%).

## Expenses

Any modifications or improvements you make in a fiscal year specifically to the home office can usually be deducted in full. You can also deduct the previously calculated percentage from utilities and the phone bill if you use a home phone for business during the workday (if you have a dedicated work line or use a business cell phone, those costs can be deducted in total). Here's where it gets a little tricky, although many tax software packages automatically account for it: if you own your own home, you'll write off depreciation for the space dedicated to business. Renters have a simpler calculation—your "business percentage" of the total rent paid is deductible. Homeowners should keep in mind that the deductions include the percentage of homeowner's insurance, homeowners' association fees, and any security services.

# USEFUL APPLICATIONS AND PROGRAMS

Working from home presents many challenges. Unlike most corporate headquarters, your living room usually won't have a dedicated IT person. This means that finding digital solutions, from efficient scheduling to team task management to billing correctly, will all be up to you. Thankfully, developers have come up with a vast range of simple, user-friendly technical solutions. These are just some of the more popular programs and applications available; there are many others. Some are free while others offer a free trial.

## Cloud-Based Backup Services

**iDrive** (*www.idrive.com*): Pricing starts with free and increases on a grade depending on the amount of storage you need. The software can back up multiple devices, such as your phone, laptop, and desktop computer.

**SOS Online Backup** (*www.sosonlinebackup.com*): SOS specifically promotes their security features that keep your files safe from hackers and malware such as ransomware. They have no free option; personal accounts start at just under $5 a month.

## Distraction Blocking

**Serene** (*www.sereneapp.com*): For Mac only, Serene allows you to customize website and application blocking so that you can only jump on social media or other time-wasters for limited periods during the day.

**Cold Turkey** (*www.getcoldturkey.com*): For all platforms, Cold Turkey calls itself "the toughest website blocker on the Internet" and aims to make it difficult for you to reverse settings; it reinforces productive behavior and reforms habits.

## Document Signing

**Adobe Fill and Sign** (*www.acrobat.adobe.com/us/en/mobile/fill-sign-pdfs.html*): This free app allows you to sign contracts and other documents—and fill out forms in PDF format—on cell phones and tablets.

**Docusign** (*www.docusign.com*): Docusign is a subscription-based service that works best for professionals such as lawyers, talent managers, or salespeople who regularly need to sign and return forms but don't want the time and hassle of printing and scanning those forms.

## File Sharing

**Dropbox** (*www.dropbox.com*): Like most cloud-based storage services, this one offers users a certain amount of free storage space and has a graduated pricing plan for additional storage. It's easy to upload or download files and invite others to view and/or edit them.

**Box** (*www.box.com*): A direct competitor to Dropbox, Box offers free storage to start, as well as a host of pricing plans to increase storage and features.

## Office Programs

**Google Docs/Sheets/Calendar:** Although some workers are leery of putting all their work in the cloud, Google makes it easy and relatively secure. Google Docs is a Microsoft Word replacement, and Google Sheets is meant to be used in place of Excel. Although the programs offer slightly fewer features than their Microsoft competitors, Docs and Sheets are free and can convert from and to Word and Excel (and other) file formats.

## Project/Workflow Management

**Basecamp** (*www.basecamp.com*): This is a time-tested team project management tool that offers an all-in-one command center for team-based projects small and large. The program allows team members to communicate, submit and organize digital files and documents, and much more.

**Trello** (*www.trello.com*): Trello offers basically a checklist organizer of tasks for personal and team task management and collaboration.

## Task Management

**Todoist** (*www.todoist.com*): If you're the type who likes to make to-do lists and you're also the type who loves technology, Todoist may be the app for you. It's essentially just as it sounds: a digital to-do list generator and manager.

## Video Meetings

**Zoom** (*www.zoom.us*): Zoom shot up in popularity during the COVID-19 epidemic, and that popularity shows no sign of ebbing. The program allows a nearly unlimited number of users to participate in an online meeting, and its popularity has been driven by intuitive and easy-to-use features.

**Slack** (*www.slack.com*): Consider Slack a chat-based teamworking environment coupled with a suite of project and communication management tools.

## Scan Management

**Adobe Scan** (*www.acrobat.adobe.com/us/en/mobile/scanner-app.html*): This handy, cutting-edge app allows you to scan by taking a picture of just about any document, from handwritten notes to official contracts. You can then manipulate the scans inside the program and export them to your computer.

**FileCenterDMS** (*www.filecenterdms.com*): This program helps you set up a scanned document organization system; it also integrates with cloud-based services to enable you to store uploaded scans safely away from your computer. It includes an optical character recognition (OCR) function that allows you do a text search of your PDF documents.

**PDFpen** (*www.smilesoftware.com/pdfpen*): Although not strictly a scanning program, this software allows you to work with scanned PDF documents. You can convert them from read-only to live text, edit them, draw on or sign them with a pencil tool, and more.

## Tax Deduction

**IRS Home Office Tax Deduction page** (*www.irs.gov/businesses/small-businesses-self-employed/home-office-deduction*)

## Time Management

**Timecamp** (*www.timecamp.com*): This one works best for anyone who has to regularly bill clients by the hour. It can also be a great way to check how long projects take so that you can adjust your billing accordingly.

**RescueTime** (*www.rescuetime.com*): A useful tool for home-based workers who want to be as efficient as possible, RescueTime automatically tracks time spent on social media sites, work documents, and other digital locations—all without you manually entering anything. It will also prompt you to log time spent offline so that you have a concise record of how much time you spend where.

**Clockify** (*www.clockify.me*): Clockify is for teams largely what RescueTime is for individuals. The app tracks work tasks for a number of workers on a team so that you can see what everyone is working on and how long it is taking them. This can be useful for project billing and team reviews. Times and tasks are entered manually.

# SECURITY

You don't need to be a contractor for the CIA to have security concerns about your home workspace. Even a basic computer setup in a home office can represent an investment of thousands of dollars. You may regularly deal with sensitive or confidential documents, from a client's banking information to trade secrets the company you work for relies on for their business success. In any case, you can never have too much home office security.

### Alarm versus security system

Home security ranges from basic to complex and from relatively inexpensive (a couple hundred dollars) to incredibly pricey (thousands of dollars). The expense is determined by the complexity of the system and the type of monitoring. The least expensive option is a simple burglar alarm wired into contacts on exterior windows and doors. When one of those contacts is broken while the system is armed, it triggers a siren or horn. This is meant to scare away intruders and thieves, but experienced burglars will not be dissuaded by an audible alarm. If it is late at night and the burglar knows you're away from home, a loud, disorienting noise is not a deterrent in and of itself because the professional criminal can be in and out of the house in a matter of seconds.

That's why "central station" alarm systems, and any with a monitoring feature, are more likely to be effective in securing not only your home office, but the entire house. A key benefit to monitored systems is that the surveillance detects not only break-ins, but fires and flooding. More sophisticated services have battery backups so that they will keep operating in the event of a power outage, as well as 24-hour monitoring so you never have to worry about leaving your home or home office unprotected. The initial cost of the system isn't the only expense; there is a monthly fee to maintain the monitoring.

An alarm such as this central station keypad covers not only the exterior entry points, but is also an alert for fire. A panic code can be used in the event that you detect an intruder in the home while you're there. Many central station alarms can also be connected to home security cameras.

## Wireless watching

These days, you can easily install your own home surveillance system. From nanny cams to doorbell video transmitters, there is an electronic video solution for any home or home office. Even old-fashioned exterior security cameras have gone wireless and high tech. Although these systems can record video to an external hard drive on the premises, you also have the modern option of transmitting video to a cloud account for a modest monthly space fee. In either case, mid- to high-end wireless home security cameras can be viewed on a cell phone app. That's all great, but there is one big difference between a network of home security devices recording activity in and around your property and an all-in-one third-party service: your doorbell cam is not going to call the police when it sees suspicious activity.

## Local protection

You can also take steps to secure your home office electronics and valuables in less digital ways. Many different computer locks are available, but all function in pretty much the same way. A cut-resistant cable is attached to the frame of the computer (or a peripheral such as a monitor or printer), and the other end is bolted to the desk, floor, or other solid surface. Many safes, for their part, can be bolted to flooring or wall studs. There are even locks, some with built-in alarms, for laptop computers. You'll also find computer "lockers" for CPUs and servers—steel containers into which the devices are secured. Physical security measures like these are excellent complements to electronic security.

Home cameras continue to fall in price and improve in quality. A professional-quality camera such as this will provide secure images night and day, but you can also buy wireless versions that will stream to your computer or phone any time motion activates the camera.

## Financial ramifications

It's important to insure your home office setup. That means checking your homeowner's insurance to verify that it covers home office computers, peripherals, and other equipment, and adding a rider if your current policy does not cover those valuables. Any additional cost may be slightly offset, however, if you have a security system in place—especially if that system covers the rest of house as well as the home office. Some percentage of the cost of security hardware and services is deductible if you use your home office full-time and it meets all the criteria for deductibility according to IRS guidelines.

# RESOURCES

## Furniture

### Closet Factory
*www.closetfactory.com*
Custom closets and home office storage.

### Herman Miller
*www.hermanmiller.com*
Chic, modern, ergonomically designed chairs, desks, and accessory office furniture.

### KraftMaid
*www.kraftmaid.com*
Handcrafted cabinets and storage features for the home office.

### Prepac Manufacturing, Ltd.
*www.prepacmfg.com*
Full range of home office furnishings, including desk and storage pieces, and wall-mounted all-in-one units.

### Webber Coleman Woodworks
*www.webbercolemanwoodworks.com*
Fine custom cabinetry, woodworking, and design services.

### Wellborn Cabinet
*www.wellborn.com*
Fine cabinetry made to order.

## Lighting

### LUX LED Lighting
*www.luxledlights.com*
High-end desk, floor, and hanging LED lights, many with integral chargers and ports.

## Paint

### Behr
*www.behr.com*
Full spectrum of paint colors and finishes.

### Sherwin-Williams
*www.sherwin-williams.com*
Complete palette of paint colors and finishes.

## Sheds

### Kanga Room Systems
*www.kangaroomsystems.com*
Varied turnkey sheds in cottage or modern styles.

### Modern-Shed
*www.modern-shed.com*
Modern-style sheds in a variety of styles and in many different window configurations and features.

## Technology

### StarTech.com
*www.startech.com*
Full range of electronic accessories for the home office, from monitor mounts to USB docks and more.

### UT Wire
*www.ut-wire.com*
Cable management and organization accessories.

# PHOTO CREDITS

Abbreviations: SS = photo courtesy of Shutterstock.com and the respective creator; t = top; b = bottom; l = left; r = right; m = middle

Pages 2–3: Photo courtesy of Behr, www.behr.com, (800) 854-0133

Page 4: Photo courtesy of Herman Miller, Inc., www.hermanmiller.com, 616-654-3000

Page 6: SS/Artazum

Page 7: Photo courtesy of Modern-Shed, Inc., www.modern-shed.com; photographer: Dominic Arizona Bonuccelli

Page 8: SS/Artazum

Page 9 t: SS/Photographee.eu

Page 9 b: SS/Photographee.eu

Page 10 t: SS/Artazum

Page 10 bl: Photo courtesy of Modern-Shed, Inc., www.modern-shed.com; photographer: Dominic Arizona Bonuccelli

Page 10 br: Photo courtesy of Modern-Shed, Inc., www.modern-shed.com; photographer: Dominic Arizona Bonuccelli

Page 11 t: SS/Artazum

Page 11 b: SS/Rodenberg Photography

Page 12 t: SS/jason cox

Page 12 b: SS/Artazum

Page 13 t: SS/AnnaStills

Page 13 b: SS/Artazum

Page 14 t: SS/Photographee.eu

Page 14 b: SS/ppa

Page 15 t: SS/Qiwen

Page 15 b: Photo courtesy of Closet Factory, www.closetfactory.com, (800) 838-7995

Page 17: SS/SeventyFour

Page 18 t: SS/Andrey_Popov

Page 18 b: SS/XaviArt

Page 19: Photo courtesy of Behr, www.behr.com, (800) 854-0133

Page 20: Photo by Jonathan Nicholson for LUX LED Lighting, www.luxledlights.com

Page 21: Photo courtesy of Behr, www.behr.com, (800) 854-0133

Page 22: Photo courtesy of Closet Factory, www.closetfactory.com, (800) 838-7995

Page 23: SS/ThreeDiCube

Page 24: Photo courtesy of Behr, www.behr.com, (800) 854-0133

Page 25 t: SS/DimaBerlin

Page 25 b: SS/Arnon.ap

Page 26: Photo courtesy of Wellborn Cabinet, Inc., www.wellborn.com, (800) 762-4475

Page 27: SS/Dariusz Jarzabek

Page 28 t: SS/Photographee.eu

Page 28 b: SS/Photographee.eu

Page 29 and front cover: Photo courtesy of Behr, www.behr.com, (800) 854-0133

Page 30: Photo courtesy of Rossington Architecture, rossingtonarchitecture.com, (415) 552-4900

Page 31: Illustration by the author

Page 32: Photo by Tone Images; builder: Gagne Construction; design by Orange Moon Interiors, orangemooninteriors.com, (941) 726-9962

Page 33 and back cover tl: Photo by Christopher Stark; design by Applegate Tran Interiors, www.applegatetran.com, (415) 487-1241

Page 34: SS/MJTH

Page 35: Photo courtesy of KraftMaid, www.kraftmaid.com, (888) 562-7744

Page 36: SS/Kuznetsov Dmitriy

Page 37: SS/-Taurus-

Page 38: Photo courtesy of Revealing Redesign, www.revealingredesign.com, (484) 840-3542

Page 39: SS/Photographee.eu

Page 40: SS/Artazum

Page 41: Photo courtesy of Historic Shed, historicshed.com, (813) 333-2249

Page 42 t: Photo by Bill Lyons, courtesy of Hammer Architects, hammerarchitects.com, (617) 876-5121

Page 42 b: SS/Uesiba

Page 43 main: Photo courtesy of Modern-Shed, Inc., www.modern-shed.com; photographer: Dominic Arizona Bonuccelli

Page 43 inset: Photo courtesy of Modern-Shed, Inc., www.modern-shed.com; photographer: Dominic Arizona Bonuccelli

Page 44: SS/BondRocketImages

Page 45: Photo courtesy of Kanga Room Systems, www.kangaroomsystems.com, (512) 777-1383

Page 46: Photo by StudioShed, www.studio-shed.com, (888) 900-3933

Page 47 t: SS/Hello_ji

Page 47 b: SS/Pla2na

Page 48: SS/Oleksandr_Delyk

Page 49: SS/Artazum

Page 50: SS/FOTOGRIN

Page 51: Illustration by the author

Page 52: SS/tele52

Page 53: SS/pikcha

Page 54: SS/terng99

Page 55: SS/Vectorpocket

Page 56: SS/tele52

Page 57 t: SS/tele52

Page 57 b: SS/Sunndayz

Page 58: SS/ISOVECTOR

Page 59 and back cover tr: SS/tele52

Page 60: SS/Borodatch

Page 61: SS/IgorMass

Page 62: SS/terng99

Page 63: SS/tele52

Page 64 l: Illustration by Chris Morrison

Page 64 r: SS/Artazum

Page 65 l: Illustration by Chris Morrison

Page 65 r: Photo courtesy of Herman Miller, Inc., www.hermanmiller.com, 616-654-3000

Page 66 t: Illustration by Chris Morrison

Page 66 b: SS/Artazum

Page 67 t: Illustration by Chris Morrison

Page 67 b: SS/David Hughes

Page 68: Photo courtesy of Prepac Manufacturing, Ltd., www.prepacmfg.com, (800) 665-1266

Page 69 tl: Photo courtesy of Webber Coleman Woodworks, www.webbercolemanwoodworks.com, (706) 769-9150; photographer: Rustic White Interiors

Page 69 tr: SS/FabrikaSimf

Page 69 b: SS/Followtheflow

Page 70 l: SS/Tanyapatch

# ABOUT THE AUTHOR

Chris Peterson spent 20 years as an editor before leaving publishing to write full time. He is currently a writer, ghostwriter, and editor. He has written more than 40 books, including cookbooks, memoirs, how-to guides, and home improvement titles. His books include several in the Black and Decker's® *Complete Guide Series*, *Deck Ideas You Can Use*, *Camper Rehab*, and *Practical Projects for Self-Sufficiency*. He currently works from his own home office in a small town in Southern Oregon. When he's not writing, Chris enjoys hiking, community service, and rooting for the Yankees.

# INDEX

# PRAISE FOR *HOME OFFICE SOLUTIONS*